Your Wife
Can Be Your
Best
Friend

Your Wife Can Be Your Best Friend

A Practical Guide for Husbands

CLARENCE SHULER

MOODY PRESS

CHICAGO

Chapter 6, "Fulfilling Every Woman's Dream," was revised from "One of God's Greatest Gifts to Man" in *Building the Kingdom in Families* (a publication of Covenant Marriages Ministry), vol. 11, no. 4, August 1998, pp. 2, 11. Used by permission.

All Scripture quotations, unless indicated, are taken from the *Holy Bible: New International Version.*® NIV.® Copyright © 1973, 1978, 1984 by International Bible Society. Used by permission of Zondervan Publishing House. All rights reserved.

The "NIV" and "New International Version" trademarks are registered in the United States Patent and Trademark Office by International Bible Society. Use of either trademark requires permission of International Bible Society.

Scripture quotations marked KJV are taken from the King James Version.

Scripture quotations marked NASB are taken from the *New American Standard Bible,* © 1960, 1962, 1963, 1968, 1971, 1972, 1973, 1975, 1977, and 1995 by The Lockman Foundation, La Habra, Calif. Used by permission.

Library of Congress Cataloging-in-Publication Data

Shuler, Clarence.
     Your wife can be your best friend : a practical guide for husbands / Clarence Shuler.
        p.cm.
     ISBN 0-8024-3188-7 (treade paper)
      1. Marriage. 2. Marriage--Religious aspects. 3. Man-woman relationships. I. Title.

HQ801 .S56 2000
306.872--dc21

99-058005

3 5 7 9 10 8 6 4

Printed in the United States of America

Dedicated to
My *Best* Friend
Brenda

When we first married, I knew beyond a shadow of a doubt that it was God's will for us to be husband and wife, but I did not think of you in terms of being my best friend.

The longer we are married, the more clearly I see why God put us together. More and more of your abilities and gifts surface. You are an incredibly gifted woman. I have learned much about integrity, character, and stability from you.

I want to thank you for agreeing years ago to do marriage seminars together. Doing them together laid a foundation for our marriage. I think we both know it has helped both of us to try to practice more effectively what we preach about marriage. I am grateful for your patience with me, because you know I am a slow learner.

Thanks most of all for being my best friend. You are always near. You are constantly giving of yourself. Thanks for saying things I don't want to hear, but need to hear. I can share my greatest dreams as well as my greatest fears with you. God seems to always give you words of wisdom for each of those situations. Thanks for believing in and encouraging me in everything I attempt to do. This book could not have been written without you.

These years together do keep getting better and better. I pray Christina, Michelle, and Andrea will develop these qualities from you, which will make them wives their future husbands won't be able to live without.

I Love You,
Clarence

CONTENTS

FOREWORD

_____ $\mathcal{I}$ have known Clarence Shuler for more than thirty years. I was with him the night he gave his life to Christ. I watched him grow as a teenager. Together we played basketball, studied the Scriptures, talked, played basketball, and then talked some more. (I hate to admit it, but from the beginning he was a better basketball player than I.) He became my "other son," and our children view him as a brother. We watched him go off to college and later go around the world playing for Sports Ambassadors (formerly Venture for Victory). Then he went off to seminary, where he met Brenda, for whom he had prayed for years without knowing who she was.

For the past fifteen years, I have watched Clarence and Brenda do the hard work of building their marriage. We have visited in their home and they in ours. One thing that impresses me about them is that their relationship is authentic. No wearing of masks, no claiming perfection, no holier-than-thou attitudes. As you read *Your Wife Can Be Your*

Best Friend, you will sense this authenticity. No preaching here—just one man discussing with other men how to have a good marriage.

I am convinced that most women want to be their husbands' best friends. The problem is that many husbands don't know how to foster friendship. It is not that we don't want to be close to our wives; it is that we don't know how. Clarence has done a good job of spelling out the basics and the pitfalls to avoid. The husband who reads and heeds will take giant steps in improving his marriage.

I was also encouraged to see that Clarence deals with the other major hurdle to marital intimacy—self-centeredness. We are all afflicted with the malady. By nature we see our way as the right way. We want our needs met first. "Be nice to me and then I'll be nice to you" is our theme. Most of us blame our wives for any problems that exist in our marriages. This is not a disease that will cure itself with the passing of time. It requires professional help from the divine healer. Clarence points the way to healing.

I am deeply convinced that husbands hold the keys to good marriages. It is my prayer that this book will help thousands of husbands to use those keys to unlock the hearts of their wives.

Gary D. Chapman

A WORD FROM MY WIFE

*W*hen Clarence and I were first married, we were friends and I knew that he loved me, but I wouldn't say that I was his *best* friend. After our wedding, I moved to a new city and state. He had already been living there for two years and knew many people. Several of them were close friends of his and some even best friends. They were the ones he talked to on the phone, wanted to go visit, and in whom he confided struggles he had encountered.

Because I was new to the place and knew nobody, Clarence became my best friend. He was the one with whom I wanted to do things and discuss struggles. As time went on, I made other friends, but Clarence remained my closest one.

Now, after years of working on our relationship, talking things out, and trying to understand each other, *I* feel that I am also *his* best friend. He still has buddies he enjoys, but I don't feel that they are more important than I am. I know, now, that there are things that Clarence shares with me that are special between the two of us because of our friendship.

He has written this book with the hope of encouraging a husband to look at the relationship he has with his wife. Are there other people or things in his life that hinder her from being *his* best friend? This book does not address the question of whether or not she has friends who are closer than her husband. Other books are addressed to women on having their husbands as *their* best friends. Clarence's hope is that a husband who reads this will allow his wife to get close to him and let his wife be the best friend he has. Perhaps in the process, he might become one of her better friends.

Let me clarify "best friends." This best-friend thing does not mean that you have to do everything together to the exclusion of being close to any other people. That could be suffocating and extremely unhealthy to any relationship! As an example, I am *not* Clarence's tennis buddy. He has several other people he can call and go play with. They have fun together and I think that is great. Likewise, he does not enjoy shopping. I am better off doing that without him! That doesn't mean that we have a strain in our relationship or that we are not as close as we should be; it just means that there are some areas in which we are different, and if we can do those things with other friends, fine.

For most wives, in order for a woman to believe that she is her husband's best friend, it is important that she feel that she is *number one* in his life. She usually wants to know that her husband values her not only because of all the things she does for him, but because of who she is. It is probably also important to her that her husband feels close to her and that she knows she is his friend as well as lover, mother of his children, housekeeper, or whatever. It has nothing to do with being possessive, jealous, or power hungry. It is only a matter of a husband and wife's being as emotionally close as God intended.

In this book, Clarence makes suggestions that have worked in our own relationship. We have learned from our mistakes, from the examples of others, and by trial and error. These are also things we have noticed over the years as we have done marriage seminars together and counseled with couples on individual bases. Many of these points are simple biblical principles, which are always valuable.

As the wife of the author, I affirm him and his writings. I believe that the relationship you have with your wife will be enhanced by following his recommendations. I know that my husband values me. He shows me by his actions, he tells me, and I know he means it. I also know that, even though he has other friends, I am his best friend.

Brenda Shuler

ACKNOWLEDGMENTS

_D_ear Brenda, truly you are my best friend. I couldn't have written this book without you. Thanks so much for your patience with me.

I am grateful to God for the parents He gave me, Clarence Sr. and Jerleane Shuler. They set a biblical example for me to see commitment lived out on a daily basis. They laid the foundation for much of what I do in my marriage with Brenda. Thank You.

Christina, Michelle, and Andrea—again you wonderful ladies have sacrificed time we could have had together so I could write this book. May God bless you richly for your generosity.

Thank you, Gary and Karolyn Chapman, for making me part of your family since my teenage years and allowing me to see the example of your marriage up close and personal.

Bob and Jean Cook, John and Betty Bass, Mark and Shirley Corts— you continue to influence me with the godly legacy of your families.

Jim and Kim Turner, your love for Christ and each other blesses Brenda and me. Thanks for being godparents for our girls.

Jerald and Jerra January and Michael and Yvonne Jones, your marriages have been such an example of grace, oneness, and strength when faced with injustice.

Fred and Mary Alice Smith, I pray that Brenda and I will have a relationship like you two if God should allow our life together to blossom for so many years as He has yours.

David and Robin Guy, Living Stones Fellowship, Development Associates International, thanks for embracing Brenda and me, supporting us in all we do and attempt to do.

Pastor Alvin and Carmel Simpkins, thanks for your example and encouragement of prayer in marriage and your contribution to chapter 5, Prophet, Priest, or Bum.

Northview Church, thanks for being the spiritual life-giving support base for Brenda and me. Jon and Beth Gaus, we love partnering in ministry with you.

Pastor Don and Mrs. Sharp, thanks for all of the love, mentoring, and opportunities to minister.

Pastor Clarence and Mrs. Hopson, Jim and Angie Ryan, Gary and Jean Jennings, Ferrell and Trese Foster, Darryl and Stephanie Moore, Dr. Malcolm H. and Mrs. Newton, Urban and Loretta Green, Don and Shelly Kentner, Bob and Sharon Matthieu, Bill and Vickie Markham, the Bill Devlin family, Dr. and Mrs. Willie Richardson, Mr. and Mrs. Will Chevalier, Dave and Tami Thornton, and my prayer partners—God has used all of you to teach so much.

Michael and Alisha Miller, thanks for reading the manuscript and for the positive feedback.

Thank you, Mike Saunier, for your initial editing and for an initial cover design. I love you. Ann, thanks for allowing me to take so much of your husband's time.

Cheryl Dunlop, thanks for your good ideas and final editing.

Gregg and Penny Hunter, thanks for coming in at the last minute, working so many hours sharing your giftedness to help in numerous ways with this book, especially the ideas for a final cover design and my peace of mind.

To Greg Thornton, thanks again for the privilege of having Moody Press publish another book. Thanks most of all for being my brother in Christ. You set a tremendous example for me as a Christian gentleman.

Thanks also to Manny and Barbara Mill of Koinonia Ministry.

INTRODUCTION

*T*he best man in my wedding was Dr. Gary Chapman, who is a professional marriage counselor and a best-selling author in the area of marriage. Gary also did the premarital counseling with Brenda and me before we "tied the knot."

Today, Brenda and I conduct marriage seminars all over the country and overseas, most recently in South Africa. We have been married for fifteen years, and with this experience and background, you might think that I have it all together when it comes to being a great husband.

I don't. I still have much to learn. Fortunately, God has allowed me to gain some insight into what it takes to be a loving, caring husband and what it takes to let my wife become my best friend.

Early in my marriage, I picked up a few bad habits regarding how I related to my wife. One came from the comedian Bill Cosby. According to Cosby, if you are married to an independent, intellectual go-getter and you want to avoid those infamous "honey-dos"—especially when you're in the middle of watching that championship basketball or football game—either pretend you don't hear or keep repeating "Huh!" By the third "Huh," Cosby claimed, your wife will stop calling you, do what she wants done herself, and leave you alone to watch that game.

I must admit, I tried Cosby's idea. I couldn't justify not responding, so I opted for "Huh." It worked like a charm! "Huh" became a vital addition to my vocabulary, especially in communicating with Brenda.

Cosby's strategy comes from one of his comedy routines and obviously should not be taken seriously. But I'll bet many of you guys—just like I did—may sometimes use a similar tactic to avoid interaction with your wife. This trick and other such ploys keep your wife from becoming your best friend. And when we look at the motivation behind employing such ideas, we see a desire to have our own way. Intentionally or unintentionally, I was being unkind to Brenda. Acting selfishly, I was placing my desire for self-fulfillment above meeting the needs of my wife.

As Brenda and I do marriage seminars, I have the chance to meet and talk with men from all walks of life. Many men struggle in their marriages. The question is not whether they struggle, but whether they are willing to work through the struggle to build intimacy with their wives. What is the main reason for their struggles? They are placing the desire for self-fulfillment above their calling to meet their wives' needs. Ultimately, the real issue is their relationship with their Creator. They need closer walks with God, which will bring them into closer relationships with their wives.

What are some of the things with which we husbands struggle? We wrestle with being the spiritual heads of our homes. In 1 Peter 3:5–6, Sarah calls her husband Abraham "lord" (KJV). Yet when we read the account of Abraham's life in Genesis, we see that he was inclined to do almost everything Sarah asked him to do. In fact, he found himself in serious difficulty after he followed Sarah's advice and slept with her servant in an attempt to fulfill God's promise on his own. Was he acting as the spiritual head of his house? In this case, it seems he was not.

Husbands also struggle with household finances, effective communication, and a proper or satisfying sexual relationship. The list goes on. There exists a supernatural cause behind all our struggles: Satan is out to do everything he can to destroy us and our marriages. Scripture refers to him as the "great divider" and as a "deceiver."

If it seems like the man has a lot of responsibility, he does. Leadership brings responsibility. So when I remind you of your responsibility, I'm not implying that you have been irresponsible, nor am I implying wives have no responsibility. But I want to inform and encourage you to know how as a man you can positively influence your marriage.

Marriage is the first institution God created and, as author Dennis Rainey has said, "It is God's first battle formation against Satan." The first couple lost the first battle. We as Christians will win the war because of Christ's perfect work, but we must be careful not to lose unnecessary battles. I have lost battles in the endeavor to achieve a better marriage, and I imagine so have you. We must first and foremost understand that our marriages are not just about us; they are about a spiritual war between God and Satan.

After fifteen years of marriage, I am learning to concentrate on preventive maintenance. My purpose in writing this book is to give husbands —and future husbands—ways we can improve our relationships with our wives so our wives can be our best friends. I will tell about some of my struggles and my failures in relating to Brenda. I also will share some victories, without which this book would not have been possible. These victories are the result of practical application of biblical principles regarding my responsibilities as a husband.

My marriage isn't perfect and probably neither is yours. Neither are you alone in feeling helpless when it comes to knowing what to do to improve your marriage. This does not mean you are married to the wrong woman. It probably means that you are married to the right woman and both of you are normal.

What do I mean when I say "letting your wife become your best friend"? In the 1947 movie *Gentleman's Agreement,* a woman and her fiancé were having problems. She asked his best friend for advice. He told her, "A man wants his wife to be more than just a companion, more than his beloveth girl, more than even the mother of his children. He wants a sidekick, a buddy to go through the rough spots with him. And she has to feel the same things *are* the rough spots or they're always out of line with each other."

I believe most men want this kind of relationship with their wives. I believe most of us want a woman with whom we can celebrate our victories as well as recover from our failures. We want her to be that person with whom we can share our wildest dreams and grow old. We want her to be someone who believes in us, even if no one else does. How does this sound to you?

Guys, your wife can be your best friend, and she probably wants to be. Are there other people or other things in the way: your homeboy, your career, your car, or something else? She can't be your best friend if these other things are more important to you than she is.

One last thing before we jump in: Few parents, churches, Christian colleges, or seminaries prepare men for marriage. As a result, most men enter matrimony without a good understanding as to what they should do after they say, "I do." We can't wait to have sex with our new brides, but we seldom know what to do next.

In doing a recent research project for the National Center for Fathering, I discovered some intriguing facts. Part of the project was to interview church leaders as to what they were doing to assist men in becoming better husbands. I found that only a handful of them were doing anything in this area. What a shame! Husbands need guidance.

Bishop T. D. Jakes said, "Women have an unfair advantage over men because women begin their preparation for marriage almost as soon as they are born. They play with dolls, tea sets, pretend to have husbands and children as they are growing up. So most women have a twenty-five-year head start on men in preparation for marriage. Men are busy playing sports and planning careers."[1]

So, husband, what do you think? Are you ready to begin making your wife your best friend? (If she bought you this book, the least you can do is read it, which will be a good first step.)

Every marriage is different, but most spouses experience similar problems. My prayer is that I will address those issues and that my words will be like receiving a letter from a friend or a caring family member. As a close friend would, I will not only give good news but also, from time to time, will tell you of the negative consequences you may face if you don't put forth the effort so your wife can be your best friend.

Reading this book doesn't mean your marriage is in trouble. Maybe it just needs some preventive maintenance, or a little "tuning up." Or maybe this will affirm and encourage you by letting you know that you are on the right track.

May God richly bless you as you read this book as an act of love for your wife and for Him. He created you and your wife. He is the One who gave you to each other for your pleasure and His glory. Our marriages, whether good or in difficulty, will leave a legacy for those around us: our children, parents, in-laws, friends, and neighbors. Let's make sure that our legacy is a good one.

NOTE

1. "Fire in the Rockies" conference, Aurora, Colo., Heritage Christian Center, 7–9 October, 1998.

Chapter One

AFTER SEX, WHAT'S NEXT?

_____ $\mathcal{I}$ t seems that most boys become preoccupied with sex either by junior or senior high school. Can you remember some of your first conversations about this subject? You may have even boasted or dreamed about some make-believe conquest.

Supposedly men reach their sexual peak during their high school years. I doubt if most teenaged boys, when thinking about sex, are thinking about the girls they want to have sex with as their best friends. This thought doesn't even enter the picture. It seems all the attention is on the boys and what they want. If they are not careful, they view girls as only sex objects.

Most of us mature in our thinking in most areas as we grow from boys to men. But does our thinking mature in the area of sex?

If we are honest, as the time for our wedding nears, our minds are preoccupied most with thoughts of our honeymoon. This doesn't mean we are not grateful to God for giving us a loving fiancée, but at that particular time we're very focused on one aspect of the relationship.

I was no different from most guys. I made it through the wedding, survived the reception, and looked forward to my honeymoon with Brenda with great anticipation. Brenda's relatives let us use their house on a lake in North Carolina. You know what most folks do on their honeymoon. We were no exception!

The honeymoon was a mountaintop experience! It was easy. But Brenda was going to live with me the rest of my life. What was I supposed to do next? I had spent most of my life anticipating the experience of having sex (and it was worth the wait), but I had given little thought as to what I would do after the honeymoon with my bride.

LEARNING TO TALK ABOUT SEX

In society today, too much emphasis is placed on the sexual relationship between men and women. Christians appear to wrestle with this issue more than ever. With such a buildup of anticipation, many of us could be facing a letdown if our preconceived ideas of what the sexual relationship should be are not fulfilled.

If our sexual desires and/or needs are not met, do we talk with our wives about it? Or do we discuss the problem with our best male friend? Do we blame our wife for what we call her failure to "meet our needs"? After all, it just couldn't be our fault. Or could it? If it is our fault, what happens to our manhood?

If most of us are honest, when we think about having sex with our wives, their being our best friends usually doesn't enter the equation. But there is a question we must ask. What does having sex have to do with our wives becoming our best friends?

As I have discussed the topic of sex with men, most agree that the sexual relationship depicted on TV or in the movies is not reality. Men who have been married twenty years or more often say that the sex they are having with their wives today is much better than the sex they were having in their early years of marriage. When asked why, they say, "We know each other better now. We know what our wives like and dislike." Often during the first years of marriage, some couples are too insecure to discuss what they really like and dislike when engaging in sex. Or they do not know how to talk about sex without hurting the feelings of their spouses. Many women have said that they are afraid to talk to their husbands about sex because they don't want to bruise their husbands' fragile egos. The result of this lack of communication can lead to sexual frustration.

What some of us men have to learn is what these couples who are having great sex after twenty years have learned: They talk to each other about this intimate relationship. As we begin to communicate with our wives about our sexual relationship, we are lowering and, hopefully, destroying barriers that might exist in this area of our lives. Doing so becomes another step toward our wives becoming our best friends. The natural by-product of this intimate communication will be better sex.

The idea here cannot be to manipulate your wife simply for more sexual enjoyment. The primary purpose is that you will be cultivating a deeper relationship with your wife as a person. The two of you will begin to become closer, becoming one. Men often don't understand that a good sexual relationship with their wives doesn't start in the bed, but outside of the bed. How we talk to them throughout the day, not just when we are ready to have sex with them, makes a *tremendous* difference. As we do these things for our wives, our motivation should be our love for them.

EXPERIENCING MAXIMUM SEX

The sexual relationship is the highest expression of love that God has given to men and women to give to each other. However, most of the sexual relationships shown on TV or in movies seem to be grounded on an incorrect foundation: *self-gratification.* Sexual self-gratification can sometimes lead to sexual frustration. If one spouse seeks to satisfy himself or herself without trying to meet the needs of the other spouse, sooner or later the spouse who is not being fulfilled sexually will stop trying to satisfy the selfish spouse.

If you want to experience maximum sex, then you might want to put a biblical principle into practice. A study of the Scriptures seems to indicate that being a servant is what pleases God. Matthew 20:26 says, "Whoever wants to become great among you must be your servant." It is usually not a problem for us men to serve others on our jobs or in our local churches, but do we apply the same principle in our marriages? If we want to be considered great by our wives, then we must serve them.

How can we lead if we are serving? Serving was the example of

Christ and Paul on numerous occasions. The best-known case was Jesus' washing His disciples' feet the night before His crucifixion, but many of His miracles also fit that description: from turning water into wine at a wedding to feeding multitudes with a boy's small meal, from healing Peter's mother-in-law to raising a widow's only son from his funeral pallet. Paul continued work at his trade of tent making, though he had a right to be supported by those who benefited from his full-time ministry. He also wrote letters from prison to encourage other people, changed his travel plans when he heard another city needed him, and kept the churches he had founded continually in his prayers.

Galatians 5:13 says, "You, my brothers, were called to be free. But do not use your freedom to indulge the sinful nature; rather, serve one another in love." First Peter 3:7 states, "Husbands, in the same way be considerate as you live with your wives, and treat them with respect as the weaker partner and as heirs with you of the gracious gift of life, so that nothing will hinder your prayers." It appears that the key to leadership as far as Christ is concerned is being a servant to others.

As mentioned earlier, if we take this approach with our wives, then this means that even our sexual relationship with them should be motivated by service and not by self-gratification. This requires the husband to know specifically what pleases his wife sexually and do it to satisfy her as an expression of his love for God and for her without demanding anything in return. When the wife does the same for the husband, then they experience what I call maximum sex. This is the way I believe God intended it to be. God created sex for men and women for their pleasure. Sarah testified to this in Genesis 18:12b when God told her she would have a child in her old age. She replied, "After I am worn out and my master is old, will I now have *this pleasure?*" (italics added).

No Neutral Zone

Maximum sex sounds great. It is something I believe all men and women want, but it does not just happen. The principle is the same as for receiving a promotion on a job. We have to work at it. We won't experience the benefits of work by osmosis. In marriage, we have to continue to work at serving our wives.

I have heard the following statement many times: "Either you are growing closer to Christ or farther apart." I believe the same is true in our relationships with our wives. Either we are helping them to be our best friends or we are driving them away from us. There is no neutral zone.

What can happen if we are not constantly developing a closer relationship with our wives? Read on.

Unfortunately, too many Christian men, even ministers, make their wives what Steve Farrar calls "trophy wives." Some men feel that by providing the basics of life—nice house, car, clothes—they have done their job as husbands.

If we lose interest in our wives, we can have a tendency to only spend time with them at necessary functions to maintain a certain image. When we have no need to keep up the pretense of a good marriage, then we may withdraw into our newspapers, TVs, computers, or work brought home from jobs. If our wives become dissatisfied, we may unintentionally drive them away from us and into the arms of someone else.

Too many Christian women have fallen in the area of adultery largely because they felt neglected. Adultery may not have been the intention of the neglected wife, but it can start innocently: a nonsexual hug from another man, praying with another man who appears to be more sensitive and caring than her husband. The next thing the husband knows, his wife is leaving him for another man. Don't let this happen to you, your wife, and your family. Adultery doesn't just affect the two involved in the physical act, but the entire family, especially the children, who almost always feel responsible for any problems between Mom and Dad. (Remember King David and his family.)

Continue to Date Her

One way to ensure that you do not experience the problems discussed in the previous paragraphs will be to practice the principles I discuss in the following sections.

In Gary Smalley's book *Love Is a Decision*, he recalls a story of a man and his wife who were having a sexual problem. The problem was not in the area of performance but in the area of neglect. One night the man wanted to have sex. As he sought to initiate the process of getting his wife in the mood, she got upset with him. She told him that the only time he touched her was when he wanted to have sex. He made her feel used or like a prostitute. Some of us may be unintentionally guilty of this.

Before we were married, some of us had a hard time keeping our hands off our brides-to-be. Most men are conquest driven, and once the "mission" is accomplished, we tend to move on to other challenges. If some of us are not careful, we will see our wives as a conquest that has already been made. We no longer have to date her because we are married to her. This attitude usually leads us to take our wives for granted. When our wives feel we have taken them for granted, they don't want to have sex with us. They can lose their trust in us when they feel other people or things are more important to us than they are. Gary Smalley says, "It usually takes a woman two years to regain her trust in her husband once she has lost it." Two years is a long time to be on probation. Think about it!

For this reason, and others, we need to continue to date our wives. Do the things she liked when you were dating before you got married. Take her out at least once a month, just you and her with no children and no agenda, except for her to have a good time. If you take her to a movie, have dinner after the movie and talk about it. Discuss your thoughts and your *feelings*.

God-Created Differences

Before we go any farther, we need to clarify an issue. In the next section and in other places in this book, I will try to explain some of the differences between men and women. This is not to say that all men are a certain way or that all women are a certain way. But there are some things that most men and women do differently. Brenda and I have found with great success in our marriage seminars that if men and women understand how and why they are different, it makes it easier to get along. This is because often, but not always, this understanding alleviates the frustration of trying to figure out why one's spouse does or says certain things.

We have to realize that God has created men and women with some differences, physically and otherwise. God doesn't make mistakes, so the differences don't suggest superiority or inferiority, but a need for interdependence. For example, God usually pairs a "spender" with a "saver." These differences can create tremendous chaos or tremendous blessings. The blessings come as couples understand and develop interdependence.

LOWERING THE TENSION IN YOUR MARRIAGE

Dennis Rainey, who has ministered to millions of married couples through his national Family Life Conferences and daily radio ministry, has made some observations about men and women. One observation is that the average woman desires eight to ten nonsexual hugs a day. This doesn't mean every woman, so ask your wife how she feels about hugs. But most of the women who have attended seminars Brenda and I conduct agreed with this. Many have said they would love to receive this kind of attention from their husbands daily. If your wife feels this way, try to give her those hugs daily. She will take notice and appreciate your acts of caring. Several hugs in the morning will make a tremendous difference at night!

Another one of Rainey's observations is that most women are holistic. Remember how your mother or grandmother knew where everyone was in the house and what each person was doing? When our wives leave us home with the children, we don't know where the children are, especially if a ball game is on. We tend to give our attention to one thing at a time because we are compartmentalized. But women keep track of it all at one time. How a woman is treated in the morning, then, will affect the way she feels at night. So call her from work and tell her you love her. If she works outside the home, schedule a lunch with her at her favorite restaurant. Buy her flowers—and *not* just on the nights you want to have sex with her. Before you know it, she will be initiating sex with you!

We need to remember that most of us are different from our wives. Many of us can fight with our wives one minute and want to have sex the next. But most women aren't made this way. They have to work through the emotions of the situation. Sometimes it may take one or two days for this to happen. For a husband to want to have sex with his wife before she has worked through the emotional issues may make her feel that he is insensitive and selfish. She may have sex with him, but only because she feels it is her duty. I'm sure that most of us don't want our wives to have sex with us because they feel it is their duty. Don't we want them to want it as much as we do?

SEEING THE BIG PICTURE

The purpose of this chapter has not been to teach you how to manipulate your wife for sex. If you practice these suggestions, chances are your sexual relationship with your wife will improve regardless of your motives, but pure motives will draw you closer to your wife. Eventually, if sex is your only motive, you will pay a price of emptiness.

The purpose for these suggestions is for you to demonstrate beyond words that you love your wife more today than when you married her. You also should want to demonstrate that you are willing to change (without her asking) because you love her. What's next after sex? Well, actually before, during, and after sex, we need to be communicating effectively. This doesn't mean incessant talking but constantly learning about our wives. This builds intimacy. (By the way, the word *intimacy* is a synonym for sex to a lot of men, but it usually is broader than that for women.) One of my mentors once told me, "You don't spend twenty-four hours a day in bed." Remember that great sex starts outside of the bed and that sex enhances the relationship you have outside of the bed. If there is a poor relationship outside of the bed, then sex will tend to destroy the relationship. Poor relationships take instead of giving. Sex that glorifies God is all about giving.

If we live long enough, some of our bodies may deteriorate to the point where we can no longer have sex. Our culture emphasizes the physical aspects of sex and neglects the importance of effective and meaningful communication with our wives. It will be the relationship that has developed meaningful communication outside of the bed that will last. If only the sexual relationship is expressed, it cannot sustain us in a way that will bless us in our later years or bless our children and grandchildren.

Let's glorify God in *all* we do because He is Lord of all.

Summary Points

1. Sex between a husband and a wife is more than just a physical exercise. To improve the quality of the sexual relationship you share with your wife, you must be willing to talk with her about fulfilling each other's sexual needs on a personal, intimate level.

2. You will experience more from your sexual relationship with your wife by displaying a servant heart rather than demanding more from her.

3. Husbands can't afford to neglect their wives' needs after the honeymoon. Continual attention through "dates" and other especially reserved times is essential to maintain a healthy marriage partnership.

4. Men and women are different by God's design. Understanding the ways women process feelings and thoughts will reduce frustration and tension in your interaction with your wife.

Action Points

1. Men's images of women and sex are often distorted by their own level of maturity. Does your view of women differ greatly from when you were in high school or college?

   How?

   Does your view of your wife differ today from your courtship period?

   How?

   List the differences in your views of your wife from courtship to the present.

   Is your view of her better or worse?

   What has caused the change in view?

2. Have you talked recently with your wife about your sexual relationship?

   Is your sexual relationship better as a result of this discussion?

Do you feel closer to her and more fulfilled by discussing your thoughts and feelings with her about sex?

If not, include such discussions as part of your ongoing marriage-building efforts.

3. Do you know of any acquaintances whose marriage was damaged or destroyed through neglect of one partner by the other?

Is your own marriage in danger of moving in this direction?

Examine your marriage to ensure that you are not neglecting your wife and her needs.

4. When was the last time you and your wife were on a date?

If you don't have a "date night" program already in place, talk with your wife about setting up a time of the week when the two of you can be alone in a special private setting. Don't forget to have spontaneity and novelty as part of your "date night" routine.

Chapter Two

SHE CHANGED AFTER I SAID "I DO"

⎯⎯⎯⎯⎯ *A*fter years of counseling troubled couples and conducting marriage seminars, I have come to the conclusion that women more than men tend to marry their mates for their potential. Some women believe that they can develop this untapped potential into a living reality. Believing that one's prospective mate has potential is a good thing; it probably would be abnormal to want to marry a person who doesn't have exciting goals for his or her future.

What Brenda and I tend to hear most often is that the woman believes she has married a good man, but that he just needs a little adjustment. As we talk further with one of these women, we discover that she is convinced that she is just the right person to turn the hidden potential into reality. But then we learn how frustrated she is after years of failed attempts to motivate her otherwise perfect husband to change. Her clever suggestions for change are often ignored.

These failed attempts to bring out the best in their husbands not only take a toll on the wives but also on the husbands. When they were dating, the woman gave her future husband the impression that things were just fine. He was loving her, to adapt the Billy Joel song, "just the way she is," and he thought that since she was not telling him of any shortcoming, she was also loving him "just the way he is." Some men are in for a rude awakening. After the wedding and honeymoon, she seems to change and show a more critical side. Husbands begin to resent their wives' always trying to change them, believing that these attempts at change are actually some form of rejection. They begin to believe that their best is never going to be good enough for their wives. After a while, this feeling can lead some husbands to think, *What's the use of trying?*

Such frustration can lead to verbal and/or physical conflicts, or it may lead to silent withdrawals. Withdrawing is one way of controlling the situation, but it doesn't necessarily make things better. Therefore, what's a man to do? What are a man's options? Physical abuse should never be an option; it never makes things better but, unfortunately, it occurs in some marriages. First Peter 3:7 says, "Husbands, in the same way be considerate as you live with your wives, and treat them with respect as the weaker partner and as heirs with you of the gracious gift of life, so that nothing will hinder your prayers." Divorce is not a good option, and it doesn't really solve the problem. In fact, it creates more problems in the long run for you, your children, and your extended family. God says in Malachi 2:16, "I hate divorce." God doesn't hate divorced people, but He hates the damage divorce creates in the lives it touches.

Few of us before we marry ever think we will encounter difficulties in our marriage. Verbal or nonverbal fighting and certainly physical fighting don't enter our minds. But with two people trying to become one, there are going to be disagreements. We must understand that there will be fights in our marriages. And I want to tell you that it is OK to fight in marriage; we just have to fight fair!

Of course, we naturally want to avoid any fights, so it is not uncommon to seek help from a person with experience. Who could have more experience than our mothers?

MY MOTHER NEVER TOLD ME

One of the first places for a man to go for help with his wife is his mother. After all, she is a woman, but we don't hold that against her.

Most of us love our mothers. Yet while we are going to them for help, we also become frustrated with them because they never told us that our wives would try to change us after we said, "I do." Maybe they didn't tell us because they tried to or did change our dads. Maybe it is a woman thing.

Our minds flash back to when we went to our mothers for help in determining whether or not we were in love. Our mothers love us, but sometimes they don't help us much. When I asked my mother how I could tell if I was in love, she said this: "Baby, when you are in love, you will know it." Did your mother say something similar to you? My response to my mom: "Thanks a lot!"

EXTRA BAGGAGE

Few of us realize that we automatically bring our personal and family baggage into the marriage. In addition, you are married to someone who probably speaks twice as much as you do, doesn't speak the same language, and doesn't think like you. All of our marriages have tremendous potential for chaos. Some people divorce because of irreconcilable differences, but I think every marriage has "irreconcilable" differences. Some couples, though, are able to work through the differences.

If neither one in the couple recognizes or anticipates this extra baggage, it can lead to unnecessary fights. There is a natural tendency for both the man and the woman to try to make the marriage and environment like the one they saw at home, which is usually the only model they have seen. Small things get blown out of proportion: how you put the toilet paper in the holder, how you set the table, that you leave the toilet seat up, how you squeeze the toothpaste out of the tube, how you fold (or don't fold) the clothes, how you drive. Does any of this sound familiar? Or how about the things you might blow out of proportion, like the fact that she talks on the phone for hours, tells you angrily that "nothing's wrong," rearranges all your possessions and throws away your favorite ragged shirt, or gives you ten minutes of detail before she tells you what you really need to know?

IS FIGHTING INEVITABLE?

I think fighting in marriage is inevitable, and because husbands and wives are going to fight, they need to learn to fight fair. If we are going to fight fair, we must have some agreed-upon rules in place before the fighting starts. It is difficult to make rules and abide by them once the fighting begins.

Before Brenda and I got married, she agreed to let me write our personal wedding vows in addition to the traditional ones. One of the vows we made to each other was this: "I vow never to go to bed angry with you, but to stay up until, with the leadership of the Lord, we have peace with one another." Amazingly enough, this is the one vow that people seemed to remember from our wedding. During the first couple of years of our marriage, people would ask how we were doing with keeping this particular vow. I must admit that we have violated it, but it has been fewer than seven times in fifteen years. It would have been better, in retrospect, to promise: "I will try never to go to bed angry with you. . ." than to make a vow. The intention would be just as strong, but we never want to break a vow made before God. But when we have sinned against each other in this area, we have confessed to each other and to God and received forgiveness. God, by His grace, had us build into our marriage a safeguard for fighting fair on the very first day of our marriage, our wedding day.

After we were married, we added another fighting-fair rule. This one is found in 1 Corinthians 13:5: "It [love] keeps no record of wrongs," and Ephesians 4:26: "'In your anger do not sin': Do not let the sun go down while you are still angry." Brenda and I have even found that we could agree to disagree and have peace at night, thus not violating our vow. But we decided it was not fighting fair to bring up something from the previous day or even further back. Satan would help us to fight each other by thoughts such as: *She did that on purpose* or *She knew I didn't have time to do it*. Somehow, things were always worse the next day if we didn't deal with the situation. We decided for us this was not right and that we hurt each other by reliving unresolved issues of our past. So we made up the rule that if we had a problem with each other we had to deal with it that day. The next day would be too late. Problems that are still unresolved the next day can easily turn into bitterness, which is long-term resentment. Ephesians 4:31 says, "Get rid of all bitterness." If husbands and wives are mad at each other for more than twenty-four hours, it becomes long-term resentment. This is Shuler theology, so you don't have to agree, but practicing this principle has done wonders for our marriage.

Some dear friends of ours, Gregg and Penny Hunter, told me some of their "fighting fair" rules. Here they are:

1. *Agree that your goal is to gain mutual understanding and not to win the fight.*

2. *Pray aloud and together. This is difficult when you're in the heat of battle, and it requires humbleness and submission to God. Thank God for each other and for the opportunity this difficulty provides (James 1:2–4) for you to learn more about each other and to trust God more.*

3. *Define, agree to, and stick to the real issue. Don't let past offenses ooze into the argument. Keep to the issue at hand.*

4. *Don't mimic each other. Don't say, "You said . . . ," then mimic the tone of voice you think your spouse used.*

5. *Don't call each other names or use fighting words. You know your spouse's hot buttons. Words like "you always," "you never," or labeling "you're lazy," "you don't care," etc., just incite. Don't go there. Stay in the safe zone by stating how you feel or what you perceive, but don't manipulate.*

6. *Don't yell at or raise your voice to your spouse.*

7. *Outline your rules ahead of time. One person gets to state what he or she is concerned about and actually gets to finish his or her statement. Then, the other spouse gets to offer a "rebuttal" or answer without interruption. Then each spouse should summarize what he or she has heard/understood the other person to say/feel.*

8. *Pray after you've reached an understanding. Ask God to help you leave this argument with Him. Don't take up an old offense, but*

forgive as He has forgiven you. Thank Him for something you've learned about your spouse.

9. *Reestablish your bond with your spouse by hugging and/or holding hands. It's helpful if you can even do this during the argument. It reminds you of the closeness you should have as a couple and that the goal is biblical oneness and understanding.*

The Empty Quiver Principle

Each time you have little disagreements, or your spouse has disappointed you in some way, you have the opportunity to put a little arrow in your quiver. These arrows build up, begin to become heavy, and take their toll on your relationship. Then, when you are having an argument or are frustrated with your mate, an arrow is pulled out and zinged at her. This will come out of the blue and have nothing to do with the issue you are presently discussing. For instance, you may be disagreeing about whether you should spend a holiday with her parents or yours, and out of nowhere one of you zings an arrow about the other one being late for dinner. The resentment these arrows build up is unhealthy and damaging. Keep short accounts. Don't let the arrows add up. Keep the quiver empty. As you experience a disappointment or disagreement with your spouse, resolve it quickly. If it's an unrealistic and/or selfish expectation you have, lay it at the foot of the cross and ask God to help you let go of it.

The Hunters, just like Brenda and me, use some biblical principles: not keeping a record of wrongs against your spouse and resolving disagreements as soon as possible (1 Corinthians 13:5). Make whatever rules seem appropriate for your relationship. The important thing is to have rules. But remember that having rules won't always eliminate your struggles.

Foundations for a Potential Fight

Brenda and I don't have it made. We still struggle. Recently, we were laying the foundation for a fight. She asked me to go to the store on a Sunday morning for milk. I don't do the shopping for the family, so I felt that I was going beyond the call of duty to buy milk from the store where she shops the most—a store far from our house.

When I returned home with the milk, I was not greeted by a "thank-you" for driving to her favorite store, which has the best prices, but by the question "Which store did you go to?" I told her which store, which I thought would please her. Her actual response was, "No wonder it took you so long. There is a store much closer."

I immediately said, "I don't think of all the stores in the area because I don't shop, but you always say this store has better bargains." (Brenda will drive miles to save money, which is good.) She could have suggested which store to go to, but she hadn't. We both had to catch ourselves and realize it wasn't worth an argument.

Later, she thought an unrelated matter was related to an action of mine. We simply had to talk through the problem. Both of us have learned that being angry with each other isn't profitable for our marriage.

DON'T GET MAD: TRY A LITTLE UNDERSTANDING

Our wives may try to change us after we say "I do" at our weddings. We shouldn't get too upset with them. Most wives' efforts to help us reach our potential are motivated by their love for us.

Let's look a little closer at the nature of women. "Women's rules" allow a woman to pick a piece of lint off the shoulder of a complete stranger who's sitting in front of her in a theater. And women regularly tell friends and co-workers, "Your mascara is smeared" or "Your slip is showing." These are signs that she cares about other people and wants them to look good. And this is how wives often express this feeling to their husbands.

Maybe you can help your wife understand how she can best approach you or when you will be more likely to listen to her. For example: "Honey, when I come home from work I need about five minutes just to relax before I think about anything else." (This is critical for men with high stress.) "A better time for me to talk would be _____. Would that work for you?" or "I hear you better when we're not distracted by kids and the telephone. It would work better for me if you'd say, 'Sweetheart, I don't have any major complaints, but I do have something I'd like to talk about. Is there a night this week we can hire a baby-sitter for a couple hours and go to our special place where we used to go while we were dating (or before we had kids)?'" If you can give her the sense "I really *do* want to hear you, but I can't right now," I believe most women would still feel heard. Hopefully using these suggestions will help you avoid conflict, as well as avoiding the nagging and tension in your home.

This chapter has been written to help you better understand the rationale behind your wife's actions when she is trying to change you. I think we have to determine whether our wives are trying to change the essence of who we are, encouraging us in good habits, or helping us lose some bad habits. We may need to ask God if she is right. If she is right, then we will need to ask God for the courage and strength to change.

In reality, both spouses change after the wedding. These changes include both good and bad. It is usually easier to see changes in your spouse than in yourself.

There will be times that you and your wife will disagree strongly about her attempts to transform you. Before these times occur, have a game plan for how you are going to handle your crisis. You can't prepare for a crisis during the crisis. And remember, when you fight, fight fair. Take this lesson from a man who wishes he had learned this lesson many years ago.

OK, go to your corners and come out fighting *fair!*

Summary Points

1. Wives seem to change their personalities in their husbands' eyes after the wedding ceremony. The changes may be real or perceived, but processing and accepting the impact of these changes must be done in a peaceful, constructive way.

2. Fighting in marriage is probably unavoidable. Develop some rules for fair fighting with your wife that will result in constructive arguments, not destructive quarrels.

3. Don't build up a "quiver" of arrows of resentment to use on your wife at your next fight or disagreement. Keep your quiver empty by resolving areas of contention immediately rather than storing them up for later use. Waiting can escalate tensions and make it harder to resolve fights.

4. Women's efforts to change their husbands are generally motivated by their love for their husbands. Understanding this motivation will help you understand your wife and discuss amicably her efforts to bring about change in your life.

Action Points

1. Did your wife change after your wedding day?

   In what ways?

   Are the changes good or bad in your eyes?

   List three of these changes and the way you reacted to each one.

   Have you accepted these changes, or are you resisting them?

   Have you discussed these with her?

2. How often do you fight with your wife?

   Are your fights controlled or out of control?

   Do you have a set of agreed-upon rules to manage your disagreements?

   Consider how a set of rules would help reduce tension in your disagreements with your wife.

3. Do you have an empty quiver or a full quiver of arrows of resentment?

   List any unresolved differences or disputes between you and your wife.

   Work on eliminating these arrows before you use them in your next fight.

4. List three habits or practices of yours that your wife regularly discusses with you.

   What do you think is her motivation?

   Have you told her how you feel about these practices?

   Talk with your wife about these and any other ideas that she seems to be imposing on you. Decide jointly whether or not these are helpful, necessary changes and how you should proceed with making changes.

Chapter Three

LET HER KNOW
YOU LOVE HER

_____ *A*fter reading this chapter title, you may think it's silly. But letting our wives *know* we love them is another step toward making them our best friends. You may be saying to yourself, *Of course I appreciate my wife, and she knows it!* My question to you is, "Are you sure?"

We discussed in chapter 1 how some wives feel used when it comes to sex, because the only time some men may touch their wives is when they want to have sex with them. Could such blind spots be true in other areas of our relationships with our wives?

Saying that we need to learn to appreciate our wives is not saying that we don't love them. The purpose of this chapter is to make sure we understand how important it is for us to express our feelings to our wives in tangible actions.

Let's look at a popular, hopefully imaginary, sermon illustration that may be too close to the truth. One woman who had been married for more than twenty years asked her pastor for marriage counseling because she didn't know what else to do. After hearing her problem, the pastor felt compelled to approach her husband. He told him that his wife felt he didn't love her. The husband's response to the pastor was, "That's impossible! I told her when we got married more than twenty years ago that I loved her. If I ever change my mind, I'll tell her!"

In this story, the husband probably loved his wife, but he obviously didn't know how to make her *feel* loved or appreciated. Maybe he never saw his father express love to his mother and, as a result, didn't know how to do this for his wife. He could have been uncomfortable in attempting to communicate his feelings and/or not have understood his wife's need to feel secure in his love. Therefore, it may have been impossible for him to communicate his appreciation for her.

Here is a more realistic progression of some couples today. When a couple begins to date, the man often goes out of his way to buy flowers, write poetic love notes, and show his affection any way he can. But after five or ten years into the marriage, some women are lucky to get a Valentine's Day card. And sometimes the husband who does remember that all-important date in February, her birthday, and their wedding anniversary can't understand why at other times of the year his wife complains that he never appreciates her.

In the movie *Shawshank Redemption,* Tim Robbins played Andy Dufresne, a convicted murderer who was actually innocent. He told "Red" (played by Morgan Freeman), another convict, "My wife used to say I was a hard man to know, a closed book. She complained about it all the time. She was beautiful. . . . I loved her! I just didn't know how to show it, that's all. I killed her, Red. I didn't pull the trigger, but I drove her away. And that's why she died, because of me, the way I am." Red responded, "That don't make you a murderer. A bad husband, maybe."

Did this man want or intend to be a bad husband? No, he loved his wife. But his inability to express his feelings in tangible actions combined with his drive to be a successful banker doomed his marriage. He did become a hotshot banker, but he paid a tremendous price for his success. It sent his wife into the arms of another man!

LEARNING TO UNDERSTAND YOUR WIFE

Robbins's character said his wife felt he was hard to know and complained about it all the time. She was giving him warning signals (complaining), which he failed to recognize and thus ignored. He didn't understand his wife. I wonder how many of our wives would say the same thing about us?

I realize that most married men have been trying to understand their wives from the moment they began dating seriously. Some of you may have given up, considering this "mission impossible." In some ways, women just don't make sense to men. We also must admit that we don't always make sense to them. Most of us have heard the cliché "You can't live with them, and you can't live without them." Basically, we have compromised to live with them because the good of the relationship outweighs the parts that may drive us crazy trying to figure out.

I speak often on the subject of racial unity. I try to explain to my audience that we need to understand people who are different from us. This doesn't mean that we always agree with them, but at least we will know why they might respond to an issue differently than we do. Understanding their background provides the opportunity for us to try to understand their possible confusion and pain and ultimately to minister to them. This becomes a bridge for them to teach us about themselves. I believe we need to apply this same principle to our marriages.

Defining Biblical Headship

Two words in the Christian vocabulary cause many women to respond negatively: headship and submission. As I discuss my understanding of the biblical definition with women who struggle with headship, they accept the biblical definition. But the abuse of headship they have suffered at the hands of men is what they say they actually are rejecting. I tell them that even though they have suffered abuse by irresponsible men, it doesn't negate what God has written in the Bible. Men, let's make it easier for our wives as we practice headship the way God intended. Let's look at this definition of biblical headship.

The woman was created for Adam from his flesh (Genesis 2:21–22). Then God brought the woman to the man. (Maybe this started the wedding tradition of having the groom already at the altar and the father of the bride *bringing* her to the groom.) Eve was even named by Adam after the Fall (Genesis 3:20), signifying his headship in their relationship in a fallen world. Adam's naming the animals was a demonstration of his God-given dominion or headship over them (Genesis 2:19–20). Possibly the most defining event that reveals a biblical picture of headship is God's discipline of Adam, Eve, and the serpent for their role in sinning. Even though Eve sinned first, God went to Adam first, indicating his responsibility for Eve. Adam was with Eve (Genesis 3:6b) when she ate the fruit from the forbidden tree. During the temptation, Adam should have protected Eve by stepping in between her and the serpent, but he didn't. Adam's role of protection became more pronounced after the Fall in Genesis 3:16, because God told the woman, "He [Adam] will rule over you." Thus, one aspect of headship that wives should appreciate is protection, which their husbands should provide.

Ephesians 5:23 says, "For the husband is the head of the wife as Christ is the head of the church, his body, of which he is the Savior." If we believe the Bible is the inspired Word of God, then we see in the Old and New Testaments that God established man as the head in the marriage relationship. This is not meant to be an exhaustive dissertation, but a brief biblical definition of headship.

But one of my sisters in Christ asked about Galatians 3:28, which says, "There is neither Jew nor Greek, slave nor free, male nor female, for you are all one in Christ Jesus." Scripture must be interpreted within the context that the verse or verses are written. The verse she quoted is in the context of salvation. The point of this verse is that regardless of their positions in life, everyone is equal as Christians; nobody is closer to God because of status or any other trait. The verse in Ephesians is in the context of marriage, where males and females definitely exist.

How did Christ become the Savior? He earned the right by sacrificing His life to pay the penalty for our sins. The principle we can draw from this is that headship sacrifices itself to be the head. This is why I call headship *servant-leadership*. It is about leading as a serving example. The implied meaning is that if we are willing to die for our wives, how much more should we be willing to live for them. I have yet to meet a woman who has rejected this definition of biblical headship.

Thus, a biblical study of headship draws the conclusion that those who are in the leadership position actually serve those for whom they are responsible and accountable. With this knowledge, we need to make a sincere effort to understand our wives, which is one aspect of serving. As heads of our homes, it is our role to initiate the process to gain this understanding, just as Christ initiated the process for our salvation. As heads of our homes, we are responsible to God for our families.

Here are some reasons we need to make this effort to understand our wives. First, I strongly believe we will have to give an account to God for the way we treat our wives. I draw this from the parable in Matthew about the stewards who were given various numbers of talents and who had to give an account for what they did with the talents they received. Also, Ephesians 5:22–33, which compares the husband's love for his wife with Christ's love for His church, implies that the husband's responsibility is parallel to Christ's. The fact that more verses in this passage are directed to the husband than to the wife also implies the husband's greater responsibility and accountability.

Second, we need to understand our wives because this helps us to develop intimacy with them by practicing becoming one with them. Third, we need to understand them so we can minister to and/or serve them when they need our help. Fourth, we need to understand them so they will feel free to develop spiritually and use their spiritual gifts in the body of Christ. Fifth, we need to understand them so we may benefit from the godly wisdom and social instincts God has given them. Sixth, we need to try to understand them because if we don't practice principles two through six, we will spend most of our time with our wives in conflict, and we will pass on to our children the negative legacy of having poor relationships with our spouses. What a disastrous existence this would be!

David of the Bible was a man God used greatly, but look at what happened to his sons as the result of his dysfunctional marital relationships. One son, Ammon, raped his half sister Tamar. Her brother Absalom killed him and then later had sex in public with his father's concubines. Solomon, another of David's sons, married women who didn't love God. The kingdom of Israel was eventually divided because of Solomon's sin. David was a great king, mightily used of God, but he was an ineffective father who left a negative legacy for his children and grandchildren.

Speaking Woman 101

Stu Weber, in his book *Tender Warrior,* said that a good way to understand your wife is to learn how to "speak woman 101." Think about it. No one teaches you how to communicate with your wife. Often she speaks to you, but you don't understand her. One reason for this poor communication is that you and your wife are speaking different languages. You are using the same words, but your wife places different meanings on them.

Let me give you an example. During my first year of marriage, I usually had my "quiet time" watching ESPN. One night, Brenda came out of the bedroom and asked if I was watching TV. Well, the TV was on, I was lying on the sofa facing the TV, and my eyes were facing in the direction of the TV. But Brenda has her master's degree from seminary, and she is much smarter than I am, so it didn't seem as if she was asking a trick question. Therefore, I gave serious consideration to her question before I answered. After exhausting every possible theory I could think of in the few seconds I had to answer, I said, "Yes, I'm watching TV." She did not get mad. She simply turned around and went back into the bedroom. But somehow, I felt as if I had given her the wrong answer.

The experiences I gained three years later from doing marriage seminars helped me to realize that I did give the wrong answer. I learned that she was not really asking me if I was watching TV. In fact, she was asking me several different questions: (1) Can we talk? (2) When are you coming to bed? (3) Is this show important to you? In other words, she was really saying, "I need some attention." Yet, at the time, I didn't have a clue as to what was on her mind. And I had no one to teach me this foreign language.

I have learned not only to be concerned with *what* Brenda is saying literally, but also with the *essence* of what she is trying to say. I could always win verbal arguments, because I could hang her up on what she said literally. I remember hearing her say, "That is not what I meant." I would respond, "That is what you said." Does any of this sound familiar?

Just learning this principle has helped me to understand and communicate much more effectively with Brenda. It has lowered the number of arguments we have, which were usually a result of not understanding each other. It helps me to be fair with her. She appreciates this effort. This has automatically drawn us closer to each other because she knows the motivation is my love for her. She also has made the effort to understand what I am trying to say.

Before we move into the next section, it is important that you remember that God is the Creator of the differences between men and women. I believe He created these differences to help men and women recognize that only by working through the differences in interdependent efforts can we experience the ultimate blessings He intended for married couples. Thus, the differences do not mean that men or women are superior or inferior to each other. Both are equal before God, but also obviously different.

Speaking More Than 12,500 Words!

It is amazing to think about how different God has made men and women. At the marriage seminars Brenda and I conduct, I always ask the audience how many words they think the average woman speaks daily. The answers are amusing. We constantly remind the audience, which is composed of husbands and wives as well as singles (engaged, divorced, and never married), that God has made us and that He didn't make mistakes. When the participants learn that the average woman speaks about 25,000 words daily, no one is surprised. But many are surprised to discover that the average man speaks only about 12,500 words a day.

This could be another source of conflict if we don't realize that there is a difference and understand that difference. This is in no way putting down either men or women but simply attempting to recognize the God-created differences. I do believe God has an incredible sense of humor!

The difference in the number of words spoken means that at the end of the workday, most men have spoken their 12,500 words. Therefore, when some of us come home, the only words we tend to utter after "Hello" and "How was your day?" are "huh," "yes," and "no." We may want to turn our brains off by reading the newspaper. Some of us use our "spiritual gift"—the TV remote control. If we have any skill, during football or basketball season we can watch three games without ever seeing a full commercial. Rookies with the remote can only catch two games. This is great for the guy who has had a long day, but it can create a problem for his wife, because she still has another 12,500 words to speak. What do we do? What should we do?

We need to compromise. Our wives should understand that, in most cases, we are not going to speak an additional 12,500 words. But we must also realize that we may need to speak a few thousand words more in talking with our wives. I learned this from Dr. Gary Chapman.

And our wives not only want us to talk about what we did during the day; they also want us to tell them how we felt about what we did and/or experienced during the day.

If you are in your forties, you may have grown up with a dad like mine. He loved me, but he did not show or talk about his emotions with me or with my mom. I may have "inherited" this trait, but it's one I am overcoming with God's help and Brenda's patience. Sharing emotions with your wife develops intimacy, which helps her feel more like your best friend. It was initially somewhat awkward for me to tell Brenda how I felt about things, not because I didn't want to talk with her, but because I was not accustomed to it. As I began to talk on a deeper level with Brenda, we became closer. And amazingly, I began to look forward to coming home and discussing my day with her. It became a release for me. Before this, if I had a bad day, I usually kept it to myself. I felt as if I was protecting Brenda. But in the process of protecting her, I was unintentionally driving her away.

Here's another key: Now that I have learned to talk openly with Brenda, I don't always talk first. Brenda is a stay-at-home mom. When I worked the standard eight-to-five day, I was often the first adult she was able to speak with after dealing with the children all day. I let her tell me what she did that day because I feel that what she is doing with our daughters is infinitely more important than what I do at work.

Now that I work out of my home and the children are in school most of the day, this has changed some. We have lunch together many days and talk.

This can be an enormous benefit to African-American men. African-American males historically have high stress levels and high blood pressures. One of the documented reasons for this high stress is not having a way to release the stress. A great way to release stress is discussing your feelings with your wife. Just think, especially if you an African-American, while you are taking this step toward helping your wife become your best friend, you also can be lowering your stress.

LEARNING TO HELP YOUR WIFE *FEEL* MORE SECURE

Most marriage experts agree that there are five basic needs for men and women—five *different* needs. Notice, husbands, what is at the top of the woman's list.

Man's Five Basic Needs	*Woman's Five Basic Needs*
1. Sexual Fulfillment	1. Affection
2. Recreational Companionship	2. Conversation
3. An Attractive Spouse	3. Honesty and Openness
4. Domestic Support	4. Financial Support
5. Admiration	5. Family Commitment

We need to do more than know our wives' five basic needs. One way to make your wife feel more secure—which is very important to a woman—is doing what we have just discussed. It may help also to learn her perspective on friendship. To you, a friend may be someone who enjoys *doing* the same things you do; to a woman, friendship is mostly someone with whom she can talk and *feel* close. To a woman, conflict or competition with a friend is seen as threatening and potentially dangerous. Along with small talk about the news or the weather (only occasionally sports), women friends talk about what is happening in each person's life, what is happening in the lives of other people who are important in each person's life, how they feel about those events and relationships, and common interests. If you want to be close to your wife, spend more time talking with and listening to her. Let her know what your dreams are, no matter how impossible they might seem. God may use her to help you fulfill those dreams someday. The eight to ten nonsexual hugs a day we talked about in chapter 1 also will make a tremendous difference.

One idea behind making our wives feel more secure has to do with letting them know that they are a *vital* part of our lives. If our wives are a vital part of our lives, then the things they do need to be important to us. If a wife wants the house to look nice for dinner guests, then her husband's coming home early from work to help clean up the house will make her feel he really cares. If he can't leave work early, then he might help the night before.

When God led me to start a church in Tulsa, Oklahoma, Brenda was a part of the decision. As the pastor-teacher of this church, I thought it might be a good idea to be there before the other members of the congregation arrived or at least to be on time. I also thought it would be good for the pastor's wife to be there on time. With three baby girls, being on time was a problem. It was actually a problem before we had children; the children just made it worse. As I sought for a solution, I noticed that as our three girls grew, so did their hair. I also noticed that it took Brenda forty-five minutes to do the girls' hair. Brenda never asked me to help get the girls ready for church, but I decided I should. I gave the girls baths and helped them get dressed. I even learned to do their hair. I did these things as an expression of love to Brenda, which helped us to become more of a *team*. The way we treat the children leaves a lasting impression on our wives. It also helped me bond more with my daughters. I don't want them to marry guys who are going to sit on the sofa while they do all the work (remember that everything you do creates a legacy). I do not consider myself weak or a wimp, but a man who is trying to make his wife feel loved and appreciated.

As I gave these principles from the pulpit in a series of sermons and as members saw what Scripture said, it revolutionized our church. Marriages seemed to grow stronger. Some things were no longer considered woman's work. The love that motivated these men (some of them former college and/or pro athletes and successful businessmen) won the hearts of their wives in a new way!

In 1995, at the Oscar Awards Ceremony, Jennifer Tilly made this statement about Tom Hanks and his wife: "They are the cutest couple! Last year, he thanks her from the podium and this year he thanks her again! They're still together! That's phenomenal! That's better than winning two Oscars in a row! To still have the same *wife* two years in a row!"[1] Indeed it does seem that Oscars are more common in Hollywood than second anniversaries, but Tom Hanks has made a wise start at valuing his wife. About the same time, Bo Jackson retired from baseball, giving up millions of dollars in order to spend more time with his family. My mentor, Bob Cook, has been married to his wife, Jean, for more than fifty years. All their children and their grandchildren are Christians.

To me, Bob's investment in the life of Jean has produced incredible benefits and a legacy for eternity. Bob and Jean's marriage is one I want to imitate with Brenda. These three men seem to know what riches really are.

We men tend to receive our worth and value from what we accomplish (primarily on our jobs). Bishop T. D. Jakes said, "Man had an occupation before he had a relationship." Women were created into a relationship, literally, out of man. Therefore, woman was never alone. So our wives find their worth in us. And if we shut them out, intentionally or unintentionally, it is difficult for them to feel secure, because they often feel they don't fit meaningfully into our lives.

What seems to be important to our wives is not that we are perfect. If that were the case, Brenda would have left me a *long* time ago! What is important is that we are making a conscious effort to keep them central in our lives, right after Christ, and before the children. A wife does not want to be considered a mistress, a baby factory, or someone who provides maid service.

Remember the innocent convicted murderer and the warning signals his wife was giving him? Is your wife giving you warning signals you have been ignoring? Make sure that you don't ignore her signals. Give her your undivided attention when she speaks to you.

Learning to communicate effectively with your wife is doing all the things mentioned in this chapter. Practicing these principles will help you in letting your wife become your best friend. As you put these principles into practice through the power of the Holy Spirit, get ready to receive the rewards that will come as a result. Those rewards will include closeness to each other, seeing God's work in your lives, and perhaps a return to a long-lost sense of first love. But other rewards will be unique to the two of you as a couple. Don't let the rewards be your motivation; just accept them as gifts from God.

NOTE

1. "Quotable," *USA Today*, 29 March 1995, 4 D.

Summary Points

1. Husbands need to learn to appreciate their wives by continually reminding them of their (the husbands') love.

2. The husband is the head of the marriage and the family by God's design. But that headship comes in the form of servant-leadership. Husbands must be willing to make sacrifices for their wives as they lead the marriage partnership.

3. Men and women communicate differently. A husband must learn the different meanings that his wife attaches to words, so that he can understand her true meaning in her communication. A husband should try to gauge his wife's feelings and thoughts on her operating frequency, not his.

4. Women have five basic needs, different from men in subtle but significant ways. These are affection, conversation, honesty, financial support, and family commitment. If the husband meets these needs, he will go a long way toward making his wife feel secure with his headship of the marriage.

Action Points

1. When was the last time you told your wife that you loved her?

   If you aren't regularly expressing your feelings for her now, get in the habit of telling her daily that you love her and treasure her. Begin and end your day on a note of affection.

2. How much time do you spend with your wife in one-on-one conversation?

   Are these talks meaningful or just surface conversation to "make her happy"?

   As your wife discusses her day with you, listen and respond to her in kind. If necessary, reserve part of your day for heart-to-heart talks on important issues in your marriage and lives.

3. How are you using your headship in your marriage?

   Are you a tyrant over your wife, or have you delegated all authority and responsibility to her?

   Neither of these options is correct. Identify how you lead in your marriage and compare it with the definition of headship in the chapter.

Secure your claim to biblical headship in your marriage as a servant-leader.

4. How do you and your wife divide responsibilities around the house?

Is she burdened with "women's work" that you might assist in?

Look at some domestic chores that you might exhibit servant-leadership by helping her complete.

Chapter Four

COMPLIMENT, DON'T COMPETE

_____ *A*re you familiar with Charlie Brown and Lucy in the comic strip *Peanuts?* Every fall Lucy encourages Charlie Brown to kick a football while she holds it for him. Every time he tries to kick the football, at the last possible second Lucy moves the ball. Charlie Brown kicks the air and falls flat on his back. Charlie and Lucy are constantly competing at everything. Some of our marriages are similar to the relationship that Charlie Brown and Lucy have.

A great way to help your wife become your best friend is to make sure that you compliment her and don't compete with her. Many couples, young and old, find themselves in an unofficial lifetime game of competition. It may be played to prove that one spouse is smarter than the other is, or it may be played to establish which spouse will be head of the family. But this type of competition is not healthy for husbands and wives. It might begin as fun, but it often ends in pain for the partner who is unable to win consistently. The result of this kind of competing causes division, not unity.

THE "GOOD STUFF"—COMPLIMENTS

When I speak about complimenting your wife, I mean more than saying that she looks nice or that you like her new dress or that her hair is stunning. These things are important to say, but more important is telling your wife how much you value her character and the person she is on the inside. The more specific the comment, the more it will be appreciated and remembered.

Where you compliment your wife is also important. You can start complimenting her in front of your children, at church, at her place of employment if she works outside the home, at dinners, and in other public places. The most important place to compliment your wife is in private when just the two of you are present. Remember some of the things you used to say to her when you were engaged and in the early years of your marriage? As women mature, they worry even more about their physical appearance. Reassure her. Let her know you would marry her all over again.

The primary idea behind complimenting is not so much just saying nice things as it is discovering how you fit together as a couple. Where you are strong your wife will usually be weak and vice versa. This is how you develop interdependence as a couple. To compliment her in areas where she helps your marriage, you need to discover your wife's strengths.

DISCOVERING WHAT TO COMPLIMENT

How can you go about discovering your wife's strengths? The first thing is to remember what attracted you to her, besides her beauty. Observe how she acts with you and with other people in different settings. Ask her what she believes her strengths are and why she believes those things are her strengths. Ask God to reveal them to you and your wife if she feels she doesn't have particular strengths or abilities or talents. Studying the Bible together often reveals spiritual gifts.

Another way to help your wife develop her strengths and/or gifts is to provide opportunities for the two of you to depend on your wife's strengths in various circumstances. Start small. When Brenda and I drive anywhere, she gives the directions. I used to drive and make sure I knew where I was going, but now I depend on Brenda. Another area is finance. I kept the books the first six years or so of our marriage. I just felt this was part of the man's role. I did a pretty good job of it until I started a mission church, which demanded a lot more time than my previous job. I'm not the neatest person in the world, and bills would get covered up in one of my stacks. Cutoff notices became common. I would find myself racing downtown to the main office to keep our utilities on. Brenda was great in that she never nagged, but she did ask if she could take over keeping the books because I was so busy with the mission church. She pointed out to me that it would be one less thing that I would have to worry about. This was good news. After one last cutoff notice and one last race downtown, I finally turned the books over to her. It is something she does well. I no longer worry about the finances; I totally depend on her ability in this area.

Before Brenda and I married, I conducted marriage seminars. How did I do this as a single person? people asked. My response was that the truths in the Bible are true regardless of marital status. After we married, I wanted to continue doing marriage seminars, but I wanted Brenda to join me in this ministry. To say that she was reluctant would be an understatement. She really didn't want to do it, but I believed she had the ability. I knew Brenda's addressing women's issues would be more easily accepted by women than a presentation from a man. I also thought it was something we could do together. Therefore, I strongly encouraged her to team-teach with me.

We have been conducting marriage seminars together for about fifteen years. She doesn't like to hear it, but she is the better speaker of the two of us. Comments from the seminar attendees confirm this. She has the unique ability to communicate with people of different cultures and races, and people respond positively to her. Doing marriage seminars with Brenda is one of the most rewarding things I do.

Your wife may tell you what her giftedness is or you may encourage her in some area, but in whatever area you choose to depend totally on your wife, it will build interdependence as both of you learn to rely on her God-given abilities.

Let me encourage you to see your wife not just for who she is now, but who she can be. That doesn't mean you should try to shape her in your own image. But as you become more acquainted with her gifts and abilities, your job will be to gently and consistently encourage her in her giftedness. "Encourage" does not mean force, but you may see her potential before she does. The keys are prayer and communication.

As you help your wife gain confidence in her abilities, you must be willing to be vulnerable. You must not become upset if she makes mistakes, doesn't progress as quickly as you would like, or doesn't do things the way you would do them. You often can accomplish things more easily and quickly if you do them yourself (as she can in her areas of strength). Products of teamwork often take longer, but the results are well worth the wait. Mistakes don't negate a gift or a strength. You must encourage your wife verbally and nonverbally and be willing to follow her and be taught by her.

In this process of helping your wife to develop her strengths, you need to discover and admit to yourself and your wife your own weaknesses and what you perceive your strengths to be. If you are weak in an area, more than likely God has given your wife strength in that area. (Brenda is good with details, but I'm a visionary.) This process will assist you as a couple to build a strong foundation and further develop your interdependence. And it will help you to assist your wife in establishing a healthy concept of self-worth.

For many men, especially African-American and Hispanic men, who feel they are competing in the workplace against a glass ceiling or against all odds, it can be devastating to come home and then compete against their wives. For such a man, there is often no place to rest. Constantly competing inside and outside of the home may lead to an identity crisis and hopelessness. Complimenting your wife and seeing the two of you as partners will break that cycle.

Let's look at some ways competition takes the place of compliments.

COMPLIMENT KILLERS:
TYPES OF COMPETITION IN MARRIAGE

Verbal Put-downs

As mentioned previously, competition usually begins as fun. It sometimes takes the form of a verbal put-down. None of us likes to be put down, so we look for a way to get even with our spouses. Sometimes when we men engage in verbal put-downs of our wives, we do it out of insecurity. In today's world, where the roles of men and women are increasingly becoming more blurred, more pressure is put on the male who wants to take leadership in the house, to be the head of his wife. Often, the put-downs can be an attempt on the part of the husband to outsmart his wife and, thus, earn the right to lead her. Guys, this isn't the way to earn your wife's permission to lead her. Besides, if your wife has a quicker wit, you could be in trouble!

Competition often rears its ugly head in the form of public put-downs—one spouse belittles the other in a public setting. This usually results in a fight on the way home or once a couple is home because one spouse has been embarrassed.

The belittling spouse needs to ask himself or herself, "Why am I doing this?" The answer will reveal the real issue that fuels the put-downs.

Public Arguments

Some arguments are motivated by one spouse who is trying to improve his or her public image at the expense of the other spouse—a sort of game of "one-upmanship." It's easy for the other spouse to begin to resent this, but biblical love, according to 1 Corinthians 13:5, shouldn't "keep [a] record of wrongs" inflicted by the spouse. Read 1 Corinthians 13:4–8. This passage explains what love has to do with it.

Gossip

Many of us husbands fall into the trap of gossiping about our wives to our friends. Gossip immediately forces our friends to see our wives from a negative perspective. Our friends naturally will take our side and give us the support we feel we aren't receiving at home. But gossip usually only gives one side of the story—ours.

We also have to be careful not to use prayer opportunities and small groups as channels for gossiping about our spouses. If you are in an accountability group, be careful what you tell the men about your wife. If some of the men in your accountability group are having marital problems, the support and suggestions you receive may not be objective or constructive.

Using Children as Pawns

It is common for couples who are having marital problems to attempt to force the children to take sides. This can have a devastating effect on the children and, eventually, on their children. It doesn't produce a solid, positive legacy.

Constant Criticism

In any relationship, husbands and wives occasionally need to give constructive criticism. This criticism should be motivated by love. This kind of love wants the best for the other person, and it doesn't want this loved one to continue unknowingly in habits or views that are counterproductive.

Often, however, criticism takes a different track. It is done to put our spouses down and to lift ourselves up, thereby earning us the right to lead. But we don't have to be better than our wives at everything. If we are acting out this attitude, then our marriages are not healthy. Marriage is about interdependency.

If at all possible, you should say something positive about your wife before you criticize her. This is the pattern Paul usually used when he addressed one of the New Testament churches. He normally said something positive to the church members before pointing out areas where they had erred.

Criticism, even if constructive, should not be constant. We should pray for wisdom as to what to say, how to say it, and when to say it—or if we should say it at all. Criticism is seldom easy to give or to receive, so be careful, prayerful, and sensitive before you give constructive criticism.

Resistance to Godly Roles

Competition with wives also is the result of a shortage of godly role models in the lives of many boys while they are growing up. The high divorce rate, even among Christians, translates into more single parents; and with the failure of many fathers to take the leadership roles in their homes, fewer young men are receiving proper training in how to relate to women.

The man's role has come under intense scrutiny lately, and male bashing has become popular in movies, television shows, and other entertainment venues. With this prevailing attitude, it's easy for women, even Christian women, not to feel the need to follow the biblical principle of voluntary yielding to their husbands. As a result, husbands feel the need more than ever to prove themselves by competing in their marriages.

Selfish Attitudes

Neither the husband nor the wife has a monopoly on selfishness. Competition is motivated by the intense desire or need to be in control or to dominate the spouse. Seldom do spouses consider that both will bring their own selfish attitudes and actions into the marriage, nor will they realize how selfish they themselves may be.

BIBLICAL HEADSHIP IN MARRIAGE

As mentioned previously, American culture is blurring the roles of men and women. Unfortunately, the issues of *equality* and *function* of men and women have become confused. Some women today earn more money than their husbands, and some believe that they have therefore earned the right to control the affairs of the household.

But trying to earn headship in marriage is unnecessary according to Ephesians 5:22–24, which says, "Wives, submit to your husbands as to the Lord. For the husband is the head of the wife as Christ is the head of the church, his body, of which he is the Savior. Now as the church submits to Christ, so also wives should submit to their husbands in everything." By God's design, headship already has been determined. You don't need to fight for it, but it is wrong also to see your wife as your slave.

Headship Equals Servant-Leadership

The world's idea of headship is radically different from the Christian definition of headship. The Bible teaches that "whoever wants to become great among you must be your servant, and whoever wants to be first must be your slave—just as the Son of Man did not come to be served, but to serve" (Matthew 20:26–28). Thus, biblical headship is servant-leadership. Servant-leadership implies putting the interests and needs of others first (Philippians 2:1–5) before your own.

If husbands and wives transfer this principle to their marriages, I believe the competition for head of the house would cease in most homes.

On the Same Team

Husbands and wives must understand that they are on the same team. Problems the couple have often come from the Enemy, and the couple as a team must decide how to handle the problems in a way that is best for both of them. This may mean that the husband or wife may have to make some personal sacrifices for the sake of what is best for the couple.

COMPLIMENTING AS A LIFESTYLE

I have heard it said, "If you do anything for thirty days, it becomes a habit." There may be some truth to this. The idea is to practice daily. If we husbands intentionally compliment our wives, some of us will revolutionize our marriages (once our wives get off the floor!). So let me encourage you to practice, practice, practice!

Maybe prayer should be the first thing we do. We could pray, asking God to give us spiritual eyes to see the same potential He does in our wives. Next, we could pray for wisdom as to how to begin encouraging our wives in these areas. We then could pray for sensitivity as we discuss with our wives this concept. And, finally, we could pray for strength and patience, especially if our wives initially reject these ideas.

It is critical that we talk to our wives and that we *listen* to them. After we have begun to practice complimenting our wives, we should ask them how they think we are doing in this area. The purpose of the question is not for an ego boost as much as it is for evaluating how we are doing. Perhaps one of the by-products will be that our wives will compliment us more.

One of my prayer mentors says his wedding vows over his wife every day before he leaves home. I think this is a good idea. But even if we don't say the vows over our wives, we could repeat them to ourselves each day. What a difference it could make in our marriages, especially on trying days.

Ephesians 4:29 says, "Do not let any unwholesome talk come out of your mouths, but only what is helpful for building others up according to their needs, that it may benefit those who listen." It is critical that we are sensitive and thoughtful with the words we use in speaking to our wives.

Speaking words of encouragement is a good way to build up our wives' confidence and self-esteem, and it is also good for our children. What a great example we can be for them.

Complimenting our wives will be accomplished as we husbands make a conscious effort to demonstrate our love for them through our actions and words. We will become a magnet for other people as they experience a couple whose actions and words are encouraging and consistent.

Summary Points

1. Compliment your wife often, in public and in private. The frequent practice of building her self-esteem and confidence will enhance your mutual love and cooperation in making the marriage successful.

2. Compliment your wife on her natural gifts, but also on those things that she struggles with. When her confidence is bolstered, she will perform her home-building tasks with greater zeal and effectiveness, to the betterment of the entire household.

3. Stay away from competition with your wife. Things like verbal put-downs, petty arguments, and gossip at your wife's expense erode the marriage relationship and do not enhance your own image in the eyes of others.

4. Biblical headship in marriage means being a servant-leader. Serving your wife as the protector of her virtue, esteem, and character will be rewarded in her loyal love and submission to you as husband and leader of the home.

Action Points

1. Do you compliment your wife?

   About what?

   Look for areas where you can do more, such as encouraging her to volunteer for community activities, host a dinner with friends, or complete a ladies' Bible study.

2. What are your wife's gifts?

   In which areas does she struggle to perform well?

   Find one of her gifts and one area she struggles in and compliment her on each this week.

   Make it a habit to find things to compliment her on daily.

3. Are you in competition with your wife?

   Examine the areas of competition with your wife and develop a plan to resolve this competition by praising her for her accomplishments rather than putting her down. Let her know of your efforts so that she can resolve any similar sense of competition she may have.

4. Complimenting your wife should be a lifestyle, not a chore. Ask your wife to assess how well you are doing in this area.

Use her comments to adjust your own practice of praise and support for her.

Chapter Five

PROPHET, PRIEST, OR BUM

What does being a prophet, priest, or bum have to do with being your wife's best friend? Everything.

I have referred to the Ephesians 5 passage often in this book. The reason is that biblically there is a parallel and model between Christ as the Head of the church and the husband as the head of the wife. Verses 25 to 28 say, "Husbands, love your wives, just as Christ loved the church and gave himself up for her to make her holy, cleansing her by the washing with water through the word, and to present her to himself as a radiant church, without stain or wrinkle or any other blemish, but holy and blameless. In this same way, husbands ought to love their wives as their own bodies."

CHRIST'S EXAMPLES

What Christ does will always be done perfectly. And though what we do will not be perfect, should we not also try to follow the example of Christ's headship? One of the examples seen in the Ephesians passage above is that Christ gave Himself up for the church. This was a self-less, sacrificial act by Jesus Christ, dying on the cross in our place be-cause of our sins. Could we as husbands live sacrificially for our wives, putting their needs before our own, or even going without so they can have the things they need? This is what Christ did for us. Matthew 20:26–28 says, "Whoever wants to become great among you must be your servant, and whoever wants to be first must be your slave—just as the Son of Man did not come to be served, but to serve, and to give his life as a ransom for many." Leadership and serving others go hand in hand. If we are to be heads of our homes, we need to serve without expecting to be served in return. If this principle were the primary qual-ification for leadership, there probably would not be many people vy-ing for leadership positions. But these kinds of leaders would be easy to follow.

Another example Christ models for husbands is self-sacrifice, which was intended to make the church holy. Only God can make people holy, but maybe we husbands should encourage this process by making sure we spend time with our wives in the Bible. I realize this may be intim-idating for some of us because many of our wives know more about the Bible than we do. This is OK. God didn't say that we had to know more than our wives. But if we adopt His example, we will make the effort to spend time in the Word together. It may be for five minutes or two hours. The amount of time is not as critical as that we actually do it.

Spending time studying God's Word and praying with your wife will benefit both of you in a number of ways:

- You will be following Christ's example with His church.
- It will provide an opportunity for you to learn how your wife thinks about spiritual issues.
- This understanding will lay a spiritual foundation for oneness.
- This oneness gradually will lower the number of disagreements between you because you will begin to be more patient with each other, and you will begin to think more alike.
- Time in the Word together will reveal your level of spiritual ma-turity as a couple.

• It will lay a foundation for a spiritual legacy for your children and their children.

Christ also is making His church holy for the purpose of presenting it to Himself. Will husbands have to present their earthly wives before God and take some responsibility for their spiritual development? Yes, I think we will.

BEING A PROPHET

The husband's role as a prophet can be seen in the example Christ gave us, making sure we are in the Word together with our wives. There is no substitute for this special activity for a husband and wife. This time together produces a spiritual intimacy. There is no other access to this spiritual intimacy than by the husband and wife's bonding together in God's Word. It will help you to understand each other's spiritual journey and some of each other's spiritual potential. This time together will make it easier to discern God's will for you as a couple, which will automatically lessen your disagreements.

When I speak of being a prophet, naturally I'm not speaking literally. But I am speaking of one aspect of a prophet's role, which was to provide spiritual direction to the nation of Israel. As a Christian husband, you are to provide spiritual direction for your wife. Today, it is not so much getting a "word from God" as the prophets in the Old Testament did, because we have His written Word for our primary directions. I believe husbands, like Old Testament prophets, are to make sure time is spent in the Word even when they may not feel like it. God often told His prophets to speak for Him even when they didn't want to.

BEING A PRIEST

Equally important to spending time in the Bible with our wives is the time we spend with them in prayer. One of the functions of the priest was prayer, which is what I want to emphasize. The priest was often to initiate prayer on behalf of Israel. We as husbands should initiate prayer on behalf of our wife and pray with her. I believe that prayer is not about using God as a vending machine, but about becoming one with Him. Children learn the language and actions of their parent(s). We Christians begin to speak as our Father speaks, and we begin to speak about the things that are important to Him. When we pray with our wives, we are more likely to arrive at the same place spiritually. This further enhances our efforts in being best friends because of the spiritual union that develops.

Pastor Alvin Simpkins, my prayer mentor and the pastor of prayer at Heritage Christian Center in Denver, and his wife, Carmel, have told me the benefits of their prayer time as a couple. I want to communicate some of that in the following sections of this chapter.

The Simpkinses admit to having had a spiritually weak marriage before they started praying together and for each other on a consistent basis. They argued and disagreed with each other, hoping to prove who was smarter and stronger. But in marriage, only the strong in prayer flourish. They came to believe many marriages are falling apart because husbands and wives are not praying together and for each other.

How to Develop a Lifestyle of Prayer as a Couple

The Simpkinses offer these suggestions of how to pray together as a couple:

1. *Make a decision to obey the Word in the ministry of prayer.*

   The Bible says we should seek first the kingdom of God (Matthew 6:33), and part of this is obeying the Word of God in the ministry of prayer. Matthew 7:7 states, "Ask and it will be given to you; seek and you will find; knock and the door will be opened to you." The Enemy does not want you to discover the treasure of prayer as a couple. One of his strategies is to keep you and your spouse from praying together; prayerlessness is one of hell's greatest secret weapons against couples.

2. *Make your spouse your prayer partner.*

   Tremendous power is available when couples become partners in prayer. The Bible says two are better than one. There are times in your prayer life when you need others to pray with you and pray for you. Jesus stated in Matthew 18:19: "Again, I tell you that if two of you on earth agree about anything you ask for, it will be done for you by my Father in heaven."

3. *Start every day with your spouse in prayer and ask the Holy Spirit to remind you to pray throughout the day.*

4. *Pray while you are driving.*

5. *Practice the presence of God.*

Talk to Him as if you were talking to someone in your car or home. Make God your Friend, Counselor, and Adviser for your marriage.

6. *Study the prayers of the Bible together as a couple.*

7. *Invest in books on prayer.*

If it is important to a Christian couple, they will do two things: Spend time on it and spend money on it.

Prayer is the vision of the believer. It gives eyes to a couple's faith. Jeremiah 33:3 says, "Call unto me, and I will answer thee, and shew thee great and mighty things, which thou knowest not" (KJV). Some things in this life we will not understand until we engage in a daily life of prayer as a couple. In prayer we see beyond ourselves and focus our spiritual eyes on God's infinite power, the supernatural power that spins the universe. This is the power that we need in our marriages.

Going on with God in daily prayer cannot be separated from the extraordinary adventure of being a Christian husband. Prayer is the backbone of a Christian marriage.

Couples must learn to keep their love fresh and alive on a daily basis through a lifestyle of prayer. The union of prayer will provide the daily freshness needed in your lives individually and as a couple. Your prayer life must come before your children, work, and pleasures. Never let your priorities become confused so that the blessing and anointing of God no longer reign in your marriage.

Couples must not let busyness rob them of their closeness and intimacy. They must take time for each other, time when they just hang out together and spend time as friends—without children. Couples must learn to spend quality time together with no agenda and enjoy life together.

A life of prayer as a couple will assist you in the process of forgiving quickly. The Bible says we are not to let the sun go down on our wrath. This is an area that takes much prayer. Prayer will help couples stay committed to each other even when the going gets tough.

The supernatural institution of marriage must be handled with a supernatural power—prayer.

Praying for Your Wife

Love is a decision. In Ephesians 5:28, Paul said that husbands ought to love their wives as their own bodies; he who loves his wife loves himself. You are instructed to love your wife and to pray for her. This kind of godly love will only come into your heart as you pray for your wife every day. As you pray, God will strengthen your love for her. You should ask God daily to teach you how to love her. This is a supernatural phenomenon, and only God can give you the kind of love that is required to go the distance in marriage.

Let me make some suggestions in praying for your wife:

1. *Pray for the spiritual growth and protection of your wife every day.*

2. *Pray with your wife for your children. It will help her to see your heart (your soft side).*

3. *You and your wife keep a prayer notebook (journal), and each Christmas celebrate God's answers to your prayers for the past year. Discuss them with your children, too.*

4. *On New Year's Day discuss your prayer requests for the new year with your wife, then do this with your children.*

Over the years of my marriage, I have learned that love is the daily discipline to continue in a marriage the things I did out of passion when my wife and I were dating. It is easy to love when we are dating, because we are carried along by an emotion. This emotion is based upon physical appearance, likes, fantasy, and anticipation. When two people marry, their love must continue in the hard times: when the spouse loses a job, becomes terminally ill, fails in a business, or is in trouble with the law.

Seeing Pastor and Mrs. Simpkins's passion for couples to pray, I hope you have been convinced to begin praying with your wife today on a regular basis.

WHAT MAKES A BUM?

A bum is a Christian husband who knows he should spend time in the Bible and prayer with his wife and simply doesn't do it. Being a Christian bum has nothing to do with knowledge and everything to do with obedience.

I have been a bum. There have been times I haven't prayed with Brenda. Praying with another person is not easy to do. I don't want you to be a bum. The past is the past; don't feel guilty if you have not been praying with your wife, but begin today to pray with her on a regular basis. Find a time when the two of you can pray together. If you can't do it daily, don't stop trying. Maybe your marriage is experiencing difficulty, and your wife won't pray with you. If you can't pray *with* her every day, you can pray *for* her every day.

Pastor Simpkins's prayer is what we all need to pray for ourselves.

Heavenly Father, Eternal God, I pray this prayer in the power of the Holy Spirit. I pray that You will teach us how to pray without ceasing. Give us a greater hunger and thirst for the things of God. Father, we are totally and utterly dependent upon Your power in our lives. Lord, give us an urgency to pray now. I believe You have imparted a desperation to our hearts for a lifestyle of prayer, by faith. This I ask in the name of Jesus Christ, our Lord, amen.

Summary Points

1. Use Christ's example of unconditional love from Ephesians 5 as a model in caring for your wife. Be willing to sacrifice to love her and meet her needs. Make sure she understands this too and responds in kind to your sacrificial love.

2. Develop a lifestyle of prayer as a couple. Praying for and with each other will strengthen the bonds between you and further unleash God's loving response to your prayers to build and protect your family.

3. Pray for your wife. This should be a daily practice. Consider keeping a daily prayer journal with your wife. Discuss your prayers and God's answers to prayers with your children.

4. Don't be a Christian bum, someone who knows he should pray with his wife but doesn't. Instead, develop a practice of daily prayer by yourself, with your wife, and with your children. Don't be afraid to ask for God's help in removing obstacles that keep you from regular prayer.

Action Points

1. Do you pray with your wife regularly?

   Do you pray for her?

   Talk to her about having joint prayer time, and establish a regular time when the two of you can pray as a couple.

2. When do you pray?

   How often do you pray?

   Using the recommendations in this chapter, examine your own daily routine and search for the scheduled or impromptu opportunities to pray. Put prayer time on your daily planner, but don't overlook the unexpected idle times when you might pray also.

3. How do you know what to pray for to help your wife?

   Only through a close bond with her will you understand her struggles and trials. Make a note of her expected trials today and ask God to ease her burden and safeguard her against any threatening forces.

4. Talk with your wife about the issues that confront your family and commit to your joint prayer time. Make sure that each of you understands the issue and knows how to pray effectively for God's help. Use your prayer journal as a record.

Chapter Six

FULFILLING EVERY WOMAN'S DREAM

*O*ne dream almost every woman has is to marry a man who will be a good father to her children. I'm not sure if we guys think about our prospective marriage partner's parenting potential as much as women do. But this is a critical issue for them. It is not uncommon for the perception that a man may not be a good father to be the deciding factor for terminating a relationship. For women with children from a first marriage or a previous relationship, a man's potential fathering ability often becomes the number one issue in considering marriage or remarriage. So another way to help your wife feel more secure as she is becoming your best friend is to learn how to be a better father to your children.

It is one thing to be involved in creating a baby, but a totally different matter to be a father of a child. Fathering in this context means how we help in the maturing of a child to adulthood.

FAMILY: ONE OF GOD'S GREATEST GIFTS TO MAN

As I write this chapter, I can't help but think about how much I miss my family. My wife and three girls are vacationing on the East Coast visiting relatives. One of the reasons they are gone is to give me time to finish writing my book. What a loving, considerate wife the Lord has given me.

This time of being a bachelor makes me realize what an incredible and indescribable gift a family is to a man! I miss the daily routine of the things we do together as a family: talking, laughing, hugging, kissing, and sometimes crying (with and because of each other). My family provides such love, encouragement, and stability for me, which makes me more productive for the Lord.

God our Father is a relational Being. He knows how critical nurturing relationships are to His children. God uses the relationships between us to glorify Himself as well as to teach us lessons so we can be more like Him.

I feel extremely wealthy when my family is together just hanging out. It is difficult for me to put into words how I feel when I see our daughters. I think possibly it is the same feeling in some sense that God had when He created Adam and Eve. I know that our daughters are the result of an expression of love my wife and I share with each other. It is amazing to see ourselves reproduced in life. God gives us the *tremendous privilege* to experience this process. We must not take this privilege for granted. Families are *special*.

A FATHER'S RESPONSIBILITY IN THE FAMILY

As the head of the house (Ephesians 5:23; 1 Timothy 3:4–5), the man is responsible to God for the spiritual and physical well-being of his family. Fathers are to lead as examples rather than as dictators. That's why I think a better term for head of the house is *servant-leader*. A father has several responsibilities he must fulfill if he and his family are to experience all the blessings God intended for families.

First, in order to be empowered to be the kind of servant-leader God requires of fathers, a father must have a good and growing relationship with Jesus Christ. Not only must he be a Christian, but it is also imperative that he be a growing Christian.

Second, a father is to be the "priest" of his family. Of course I do not use the word *priest* literally, as though to suggest his role is identical to that of the priest in Scripture, but I believe the father's responsibility parallels Christ's responsibility for His church. I believe the father is to be the spiritual leader and mediator (praying daily) for his family. He does not have to know more than his wife, but I do believe God holds the man responsible for ensuring that his family has family devotions (time in God's Word and prayer as a family). Both parents, especially the father, should establish set times in the family schedule to teach the Word of God (Ephesians 6:4b). These devotions lay the foundation for the legacy of a godly family to be established and passed on as our children mature and have their own families. A godly father makes it easier for his children to understand and accept God as their Father.

Christian recording artist Sheila Walsh struggled with recognizing God as her Father because of a childhood experience she had with her earthly father. Her father became mentally ill when she was four years old. This illness produced unexpected mood swings in his behavior. This once gentle, sensitive, loving father could become violent at the drop of a hat. One day he came at her abruptly. She thought he was going to hurt her, so she snatched his cane out from under him. He fell and she ran to safety. It wasn't until her senior year at a Bible college in London that she faced her past with the help of her mother and reconciled her feelings about her father. This emotional burden had made it difficult for her to have long-lasting relationships with men.

Children often believe that when something goes wrong in their homes, it is their fault. Sheila felt as if her father's illness, mood swings, and death were somehow her fault. Her mother's assurance that Sheila was not the cause of anything that happened to her father freed her to begin to worship God as her Father.

Third, a father must be a loving husband. Steve Farrar says it is easy for men to make their wives trophy wives, because we tend to be conquest oriented. Once we have conquered or accomplished our mission, we have a tendency to move on to the next conquest. This is natural for men, but we can't just put our wives on the shelf. The power of the indwelling Holy Spirit enables us to become sensitive, caring, and responsive husbands.

As a loving husband, you are responsible to help your wife be all she can be for Christ. As you provide security for your wife, this allows her to blossom for the Lord and for you. Security for your wife is not just a roof over her head and paying bills on time, but it is a process of becoming one with her. It has to do with listening, encouraging, and doing things that she feels are important. It is a partnership, but not a fifty-fifty partnership the world recognizes, where no one knows where his or her partner's 50 percent ends and his or her own begins. It is a partnership of commitment to work together. This partnership is about giving 100 percent without demanding anything in return. It requires becoming vulnerable with your wife, and it demands letting your wife know your wildest dreams, hurts, and, yes, even your biggest fears. Admitting that you have fears does not make you a lesser man. Not telling her of them may just make you appear stupid. Not telling your fears also intentionally or unintentionally shuts your wife out on a part of who you are. This hurts your ability to really be intimate. Remember that intimacy is developed outside the bed. If you shut your wife out, then God can't use the wisdom and love He has given her to minister to you. You lose if you shut out your wife.

ROLE-MODELING FOR YOUR CHILDREN

Our children learn how to be good or bad husbands and wives by watching us. The question we must ask ourselves is whether we want our children to be the kind of husbands we are. My childhood friend Steve (not his real name) became an attorney and married a hometown girl, also an attorney. In Steve's home, when his father and mother disagreed, his father physically beat his mother. Guess what Steve did with his wife when they disagreed? You would think that since they were lawyers they would talk each other to death, but instead, Steve did what he saw his father do to his mother: He beat his wife. The marriage only lasted three weeks!

Fourth, fathers must love their children. Our children need our example, wisdom, touch, and words of encouragement. We need to help them to dream. We need to help them to be able to find ways to fulfill their dreams. Fathers also need to continue to hug their sons and daughters during their teenage years. Even though the boys are trying to be men before their time, they still need the loving touch of their fathers. Our children also learn how to be affectionate from how we demonstrate affection to our wives. Often as our daughters grow up, it is their growing out that may threaten us. If we stop hugging our teenage daughters, they may go looking for love in all the wrong places and find it. Consistent, nonsexual hugs may provide our daughters with the strength to resist sex before marriage. What do you think? Is it worth the effort?

God uses the influence of men to help boys determine their masculinity, but He also uses men to help girls determine their femininity. This may be something some of us men have never thought about. Some Christian family therapists believe that the absence of godly men in the home often contributes toward homosexual and lesbian tendencies for children. This is not downplaying the importance of the mother, but I am simply saying that there are consequences when God's institution of marriage and family is altered from His original plans.

Ephesians 6:4 says, "Fathers, do not provoke your children to anger; but bring them up in the discipline and instruction of the Lord" (NASB). It is important that we don't exasperate or provoke our children. Sometimes our children's best is never good enough for us. If they are singles hitters, we always are demanding a double, or if they are B students, we demand A's.

Most children and youth want their fathers to give them boundaries. These boundaries produce security. To my amazement, when I worked for the Chicago Gospel Youth Center in Chicago, I saw some kids intentionally get in trouble so their parents—who were often working two to three jobs—would spank them. Because their parents were gone so much trying to provide for them, sometimes the youths needed to be reassured of their parents' love. A spanking or some kind of discipline provided this reassurance.

I must have been the most loved child in North Carolina because it seemed my parents spanked me every day! I was always in trouble and needed spankings. I truly believe that without those spankings, I would have ended up in jail or dead or both.

It is primarily our responsibility as fathers, not that of the local church to which we belong, to teach our children the Word of God and provide appropriate discipline. Experts on marriage and family also believe that if the father goes with his children to church and doesn't just send them, this has a dramatic influence on the children having an active, personal relationship with Jesus Christ and not just being religious. By religious, I mean routinely fulfilling "religious duties," such as church attendance, without being involved in a personal relationship with Jesus Christ.

GOD'S BEST FOR YOUR FAMILY

God has given us a tremendous gift in the family. We as fathers have an awesome role to play in the development of a family that glorifies God. You might be wondering, *What is in it for me?* First, I believe you will find fulfillment in doing what God has commanded. Second, you will have peace from God because you are in His will. Third, I believe your family will treat you like a king because of what they experience in the love you shower on them.

Let us make the most of this incredible gift of family God has given us—for His sake, our family's, and ours.

Summary Points

1. Among the qualities most sought by a woman in her husband is the ability to be a good father to her children. Husbands must keep this in mind as they begin to grow their families.

2. Family is one of God's greatest gifts to man. Fathers should view their relationship to their own children as God does to His children, with joy and love.

3. A father has several responsibilities to his children. He must be a servant-leader, the spiritual head of the house, and a loving husband to their mother.

4. Fathers must also be good role models for their children. They must provide instruction, protection, and love for their children to emulate as the children grow and mature.

Action Points

1. Does your wife think you are a good father to your children?

   Do you have to be reminded frequently by her of your fatherly responsibilities?

   If so, examine your own involvement in raising your children, ensuring that you are being the kind of father God intends you to be.

2. List the positive effects of family for you. How does your family make your life better?

   Be sure to appreciate your family each day and thank God for their presence in your life.

3. On a scale of 1 to 10, how would you rate yourself as a servant-leader of your family?

   The spiritual head?

   A loving husband?

   Ask your wife to rate you in these areas.

Imagine how your children might rate you.

Always work to be as close to a 10 as possible.

4. Are you a consistent and effective role model of good behavior for your children?

Are there areas you can improve in?

List some recent successes and failures, and try to identify how you might become better.

Chapter Seven

DIVORCE: DON'T GO THERE

*J*f you are considering divorce and reading this chapter right now, it might seem an impossibility for you to become best friends with your wife. I want to assure you that it is not too late! I believe that with God, nothing is impossible (Mark 10:27).

Most of us have been affected by divorce personally, through members of our families and/or through friends. My purpose here is to provide words of encouragement and an awareness of the truths concerning divorce. My hope is that you will be able to rekindle a loving relationship with your wife. If you and your wife are struggling to keep your marriage together, some of what I say may help you see where and how your relationship has gone wrong and what may be done to save your marriage.

MARRIAGE IS A STEP OF FAITH

Dr. Gary Chapman often says at his marriage seminars that the word *love* involves "two consonants, l and v; two vowels, o and e; and two fools, you and me!" This is a humorous saying, but it reveals truth. When most of us married, we knew little about our spouse or about ourselves. It may have been a little foolish for some of us to have entered into such an undertaking with so little preparation for the adventure ahead. And whether we realized it or not, most of us entered into an adventure of faith. In fact, any marriage is about faith. The key is in whom or what the couple has faith.

Some cultures try to ensure that marriages will last. Parents might prearrange the marriage based on what they believe is best for their children. But in our culture, most marriages are the result of some form of dating, where both partners attempt to verify their feelings for each other by spending the time necessary to answer any questions they may have concerning a potential spouse.

But no matter what you do or what has been done for you, in some sense, it seems no guarantees exist for marriage. It is true that the success of a marriage is not entirely in your control. Actually the success of your marriage is in the hands of you and your spouse.

Even today, as Brenda and I are working on our fifteenth year of marriage, I marvel when I think about it. I can still remember how *nervous* I was at our wedding, because I kept thinking, *This is forever!* On July 27, 1985, in the presence of many witnesses, Brenda and I committed to each other and, most importantly, to God that we would stay married for a lifetime.

This commitment is critical to helping your wife become and remain your best friend. In the Christian life, God comes first, then your spouse, next your children and, last, whatever ministry God may give you. Don't ever let this order change. If you do, the effects will devastate your family! Therefore, your wife shouldn't love you the most; she needs to love God more than anyone else. In the same way, you should love God more than you love your wife. It follows, then, that your marriage is based on your relationship with Christ first and then with your spouse.

If this is true, you should seek opportunities for you and your wife to grow together spiritually. In this way, you will be honoring God and your wife. Growing together spiritually develops intimacy with God and with your wife, which results in oneness. This oneness makes divorce less likely in your marriage.

Husbands who spend little or no time providing spiritual opportunities to grow closer with their wives may be considered foolish. They
are building their marriages on sand instead of on rock (Matthew 7:24–
27), and the longevity of their marriages may be in jeopardy. If their
marriages last, it may be purely because of their wives' love for God. For
these wives, divorce is not an option, no matter how bad things become.
But this kind of marriage will not provide the fulfillment God intended for husbands and wives.

"ME-ISM"—A HINDRANCE TO GREAT MARRIAGE

Some marriage experts believe that the divorce rate in America is 50
percent; some say it is as high as 66 percent. Others dispute both fig-
ures and say it is actually more like 25 percent. Whatever the rate really is, one thing is certain—it is too high! This high divorce rate
negatively affects unmarried people, many of whom believe it doesn't
make sense to marry because no one stays together anymore. They decide to eliminate the hassle of marriage and just live together—until they
find a better partner and move on. Or those who are already married
live with a sense that it's inevitable they will someday be divorced.

The most disturbing information over the last few years is that the
divorce rate among Christians is the same as it is among non-Christians.
Some marriage experts are even saying that the divorce rate among
Christians is higher than it is among non-Christians! According to
George Barna, the divorce rate among non-Christians is 27 percent,
among Christians 27 percent, and 30 percent among fundamentalist
Christians.[1] This figure can be debated, but that some have even found
grounds for saying it is a matter of concern. We can't ignore this issue
anymore as something only affecting other people. It has found its way
into the church. How can this be?

It seems some Christians have adopted a "me-ism" theology, which
says God wants *me* to be happy. Everything revolves around the person in this theology. Servanthood does not enter the picture. When
things become difficult or unpleasant, Christians with this mind-set will
say, "I know God wants me to be happy, and I'm not happy with you.
Therefore, I'm divorcing you." In premarital counseling, if a couple says
to me, "Divorce is an option," I won't marry them.

What is sad is that these kinds of sinful divorces have become common in the church. I label them as sinful divorces because the Bible does not support divorce on these grounds. The only biblical grounds for divorce are adultery and desertion. Nothing is written about divorce because of incompatibility or other such ideas. Some of you may ask, "What about a woman who is being abused?" First Corinthians 7:10–11 states, "A wife must not separate from her husband. But if she does, she must remain unmarried or else be reconciled to her husband." I don't tell women whether to stay or leave in such an abusive marriage. I have heard of Christian women who have stayed with their unsaved husbands in difficult situations for many years, and eventually they have seen God bring their husbands to Christ. These husbands publicly praise their wives for staying with them during the bad times. I encourage the wife who is being abused to pray about the situation and to receive direction from God and her pastor or a wise older Christian couple.

ILL PREPARED FOR A LIFELONG COMMITMENT

The lack of biblically-based premarital counseling for couples is making it difficult for some marriages to be successful. It is astonishing to me that couples will seek advice about buying a house or about investing in the stock market, but will not seek counsel about marriage, a lifelong commitment. Without this help some couples are entering marriage not knowing what to expect, not knowing what or how to deal with the baggage they bring into the relationship. These couples may not even realize that they have baggage.

The answer many of these couples hold in reserve is divorce. If it doesn't work out, they say, they can always divorce. Many young people today come from homes where their parents divorced. So for them divorce, while not the ideal situation, is acceptable.

They have not learned the lesson that divorce brings devastating consequences. And, unfortunately, we don't hear many pastors preach about divorce. Actually, church members often add to the problems of those who have been divorced. One of the things that saddens me is that when someone in a church goes through divorce, whether biblically justified or not, many in the church ostracize the divorced persons. This is usually unintentional. Some people just don't know what to say, so they say nothing. They begin avoiding the divorced person. In the end, because the divorced person feels rejected, he or she ends up leaving the church—the very place that should have been a haven of love and healing.

HOW GOD VIEWS DIVORCE

God hates divorce, but He *does not hate divorced people!* In fact, He loves them as much after their divorce as He did before.

Years ago, David Hocking discovered in Malachi 2:10–16 why God hates divorce (not divorcés), and I want to go over these reasons with you.

Breaking a Vow

The first reason God hates divorce is that it contradicts His original plan for married couples. In Malachi 2:10, the emphasis is on profaning the covenant by *breaking faith* with others. The idea of breaking faith here means to betray a trust, to be unfaithful to a commitment, and/or to undermine another's position.[2] Marriage is an institution that God established in Genesis 2:24. Once you make a vow to God, He expects you to keep it. It is better not to vow, than to vow and then break it (Psalm 116:14; Proverbs 20:25; Numbers 30:2; Deuteronomy 23:21–23; Ecclesiastes 5:4–6).

Some of the vows in Scripture are quite costly. When Hannah, Samuel's mother, vowed to give her firstborn to God if He gave her a baby, keeping her vow meant following years of childlessness with giving up that greatly wanted child. David and Jonathan vowed friendship to each other, which for Jonathan meant guarding the life of the man who would someday be king in his place. These people *knew* the life-and-death importance of keeping a vow made to God.

As Christians, we should seriously consider the importance of vows made to God and the consequences if we should break them. The Word of God, prayer, God's will, and counsel from mature Christians will help us to be in the center of God's perfect will (Romans 12:1–2).

Defiling What God Loves

God hates divorce because it defiles that which He loves. In Malachi 2:11, we read that breaking faith is an abomination to God (KJV). God created the institution of marriage for men and women to enjoy. It is one of His greatest gifts to us. Divorce then is a rejection of this precious gift, intentionally or unintentionally making light of His institution of marriage.

If you break a business contract without good reason, your reputation may precede you, and it can become difficult to enter into other business contracts in the future because no one will trust you. Can God trust you with your word? Do you keep your vows?

Denying Consequences

Divorce denies that any consequences will result from the actions taken. Verse 12 of Malachi 2 says, "As for the man who does this, whoever he may be, may the Lord cut him off from the tents of Jacob—even though he brings offerings to the Lord Almighty." This phrase means that all offenders would be deprived of legal protection and left without witness or a defender in court.[3] A divorce, sinful or not, seriously affects the lives of both spouses, their children, and their extended families.

The key is repentance. Divorce (without biblical grounds) should never be an option for Christians. I understand the reality of divorce and know that some of you reading this book have experienced divorce. This is not a condemnation or a judgment. Neither do I want to encourage divorce or remarriage. But the reality is that if you are divorced, you will probably consider remarriage sooner or later. This chapter may help if you are considering remarriage or are already in another marriage. Please don't stop reading. This information also may be helpful to a son or daughter or to a friend. If you are divorced, try if possible to obtain forgiveness from your former spouse. Romans 12:18 tells us, "If it is possible, as far as it depends on you, live at peace with everyone." So the purpose of attempting to secure this forgiveness is to obey God. All actions have consequences. As Christians, we must realize that everything we do either brings glory to God or dishonors Him.

Downplaying the Importance of the Marriage Vow

Divorce disregards the importance of the marital vow. I realize I have talked about this earlier, but I want to examine the consequences more closely.

Marriage should not be based exclusively on human love or on sexual desire, but on a vow spoken to God. Once this vow is made, it becomes His will for the vow to be kept—no matter what!

Biblically, Christians *cannot* fall out of love because biblical love is not based on emotion but on action. If you study Ephesians 5:21–33, you will discover that God doesn't command our emotions; He commands our actions. Dr. Gary Chapman says that the "tingles," the feelings we have the first two years or so of our courtship and marriage, can't be maintained because of the intensity of them. This doesn't mean we start loving our wives any less; it is just that emotional feelings aren't always as intense later as at the beginning.

The primary witness at our weddings was not our fathers or mothers, but God. Divorce demonstrates a lack of appreciation for our vows. Where are the people of God who are going to be committed to their marital partners no matter what?

Godly parents provide the opportunity for children to *learn* what commitment means by seeing the faithfulness of their parents to the Lord and to each other. Seeing this commitment of the parents to God and to each other produces security for children. One thing that makes it easier for me to stay with Brenda, even when I have been frustrated with her, is that my dad never left my mom.

Destroying Children

A few years ago, the number one counseling problem in America was assisting children from divorced homes. The number one problem in remarriage during this same time (and may still be) was raising a child who did not belong to one of the parents. This primary problem in these blended families is answering the question of how the children will be disciplined. Children often play one parent against the other when both are their natural parents; you can imagine how much higher the stakes become in blended families.

Recent studies of children from marriages ending in divorce show that children are the real victims when the parents split. The following are some of the symptoms that have been observed in children of divorced parents:

1. A high incidence of depression and sadness

2. Guilt over the divorce and an uneasy feeling that they may have caused it

3. *A refusal to accept the finality of the divorce and a clinging to the hope that the parents will reconcile*

4. *Bodily pains and distresses*

5. *A tendency to exhibit attention-getting behavior that clashes with the rules of society and/or the moral guidelines of their parents (truancy, running away, delinquency, poor school performance, sexual misbehavior, drug use, temper tantrums, and aggression)*

6. *Difficulty in resolving normal childhood and adolescent conflicts*

7. *A tendency to withdraw into one's own private world*

8. *A fear of forming relationships of intimacy and trust, lest they be hurt again*

9. *Fear of abandonment*

10. *Hurt and disappointment that their parents did not love them enough to stay together*

11. *A fear of their own failure as future marriage partners*[4]

In order to avoid divorce, husbands and wives need to follow the advice of Malachi 2:15: "Take heed to your spirit, and let none deal treacherously against the wife of his youth" (KJV). The problem according to verse 16 resides *inside* of us. The focus should not be on the problems of our spouses, but on us and our need to be changed by God. In many cases, when one spouse sees the other change for the better, it opens him or her up to change. We must remember that only God can change hearts.

WHAT DOES ALL OF THIS MEAN?

Divorce is an *inadequate* solution to marital problems. Forgiveness is at the heart of God, and He is a God of grace. This means that we should be people of grace. Hosea, by biblical law, had the right to stone his wife to death because she was guilty of adultery. But he took her back because God wanted his marriage to be a living object lesson of His own grace. I am not saying that everyone whose spouse commits adultery should be reconciled. I am suggesting that you give much time in prayer and in seeking godly counsel before making a decision (1 Corinthians 7; 1 Peter 3:1–7).

Our attitude toward divorce should reflect God's view. Christians should hate divorce but not divorced people, and they should demonstrate compassion.

If you are guilty of a sinful divorce, confess it now and repent. God will forgive you (1 John 1:9)—although forgiveness does not remove the consequences. Seek forgiveness from your former wife and try to live at peace with her, even if you don't become best friends. This does not mean that you should divorce your present wife if you have remarried.

Commit from this day on to never allow divorce to be an option for your marital problems. Tell your wife that she is stuck with you and that you love her. Tell her that you are committed to her no matter what! Prayerfully consider renewing your wedding vows.

WHAT MAKES YOU THINK
YOUR MARRIAGE WILL BE BETTER?

Just reading about the consequences of divorce can be like a cold slap in the face. We have to ask ourselves the question, "What is the alternative?"

You can know that in the marriage you have now, whether it is your first, second, or third marriage it is now God's will for you to stay together for life. You also can know that God, through the power of the Holy Spirit, will empower you to stay together (Philippians 4:13; 1 John 5:14–15). As we and our spouses stay committed to God and to our marriages, He is able to provide present and future rewards beyond our wildest dreams.

NOTES

1. "Reaqching Without Preaching," *The Barna Report* (Septembe-October 1996), 3.
1. Page H. Kelly, *Malachi: Rekindling the Fires of Faith* (Nashville: Convention Press, 1986), 43.
2. Ibid., 45.
3. Ibid., 62.

Summary Points

1. Marriage is a step of faith. It is not only faith between marriage partners in each other, but faith in God's institution of marriage.

2. Divorce has become very common in America. A frequent cause of divorce is an unduly selfish focus on oneself, rather than on one's spouse and preserving the marriage. A successful marriage requires a commitment of both spouses to each other and to the marriage.

3. Too many couples enter into marriage without adequate counseling. Thus they are more likely to resort to divorce when trials come. Divorce should not be an option for Christian couples, because it runs counter to God's plan to fulfill His will in couples' lives.

4. Divorce has consequences. Not only do both partners suffer damaged emotions, but children, family members, and the community at large also feel the effects of divorce.

Action Points

1. What does marriage mean to you?

   Have you thought about marriage from a commitment point of view?

   From a faith point of view?

   Write down your own definition of marriage.

   Ask your wife to do the same. Compare definitions and see if one or both of you are lacking in a faith commitment to your marriage.

2. Is one partner more important than another in your marriage? Is it you?

   How often do you place yourself ahead of your wife in meeting needs?

   Assess your efforts to place your wife ahead of you in meeting needs.

   If she doesn't fit into your cycle of fulfillment, make a deliberate effort to do more for her, rather than yourself.

3. Is divorce an option you would consider if your wife made you "un-happy"?

   If so, ask yourself how you might resolve any feelings of unhappiness with her without resorting to divorce.

   If you have serious issues here, discuss them with her in a compassionate, constructive way.

4. Have you witnessed the effects of divorce on yourself or on friends?

   What would happen if you suddenly were divorced?

   Who would be affected and how?

   Pray today for God's strength and wisdom to deal with any issues that threaten your marriage.

Chapter Eight

HOW SWEET
IT IS!

*H*ow sweet it is. This often-repeated Jackie Gleason phrase is exactly how I feel about my relationship with Brenda as I review how our marriage has grown. You discovered by reading this book that it was not always this way. Just as I said in the introduction, the satisfaction of our relationship is not based on perfection. And if you have learned anything from this book, you realize that I have not arrived as a husband. I will have to work at my marriage as long as I live. I hope you have come to the same realization. This attitude and consequential actions are necessary if we are going to allow our wives to become and stay our best friends.

The foundation for this satisfaction that husbands and wives can have with each other is grounded in each of our personal relationships with Jesus Christ as our Lord and Savior. This relationship motivates us to do things that are beneficial for us as a couple—things that are not always accompanied by warm, fuzzy emotions. In fact, they may be done in opposition to how we feel. But they are a result of obedience to God and His Word.

MAKING IT CLICK

I can remember from the first few years of our marriage, how shocked I was to discover that Brenda and I were so different. Our differences led to many disagreements. I kept thinking, *How could this be?* We never seemed to have these problems when we were dating. We were both Christians, but how could we be so different? Why was it such a struggle to get along with each other?

Even though I loved Brenda, I was unhappy with our marriage. We just didn't seem to be clicking with each other.

In the city where we lived during the first years of our marriage, a number of Christian leaders' marriages ended in divorce. I didn't want to become one of those casualties of divorce. I knew God loved divorced people, but I also knew He hates divorce (Malachi 2:16). I knew marriage was supposed to be forever. My parents stayed together until death separated them. I knew the Bible's teaching on divorce, and I had my parents' positive example of how to stay together.

I didn't blame Brenda for my struggle, even though I felt she contributed to it. As the head of the house, I felt, I knew somehow, that the problem was with me. And it was my responsibility to solve the problem. I asked Brenda to go with me to a Dennis Rainey Family Life Conference. I simply told her I needed help with our marriage, and she agreed to go.

Stu Weber and Steve Farrar spoke at the conference, telling the mistakes they made in their marriages and how they worked through them with their wives. I could hardly believe that these two godly men talked about the same things I was experiencing, such as how to communicate with Brenda, how practically to be head of the house (what did it really mean), coping with my very intelligent and independent wife, etc. The conference helped me to learn how to communicate more effectively with Brenda, and it helped me to see that some of the mistakes I was making were normal and could be corrected.

The time was for me a landmark in our marriage. The information I received didn't eliminate our problems, but it gave me confidence to believe that I could have a satisfying marriage. It also encouraged me to begin to practice more effectively working through problems with Brenda. For example, when I would get ready to leave home, Brenda wanted to know where I was going and when I would return. I remembered this same question from my mother. I didn't realize at first that this helped Brenda feel secure by letting her know where I was in case I got hurt or she had an emergency. Initially, I incorrectly felt she was trying to control me. Then I realized that if I loved her, it wasn't a big deal to inform her of my whereabouts.

Then Gary Chapman, our premarital counselor, helped Brenda and me to see that our marriage made us a team. God had brought us together, but Satan was trying to drive us apart. Gary told us we should view the problem as our enemy and see that we were on the same side. We had to decide what was best for us as a *couple*. This may require personal sacrifice by one of us as an individual for the good of the couple.

Rewards

Armed with the above knowledge, Brenda and I began to see our marriage improve—and we felt God leading us to tell others what we learned. Soon, Brenda joined me in doing marriage seminars, doing them for people who couldn't afford to attend a conference or who had no concept of what a marriage seminar is. We spoke not as experts (we aren't experts today), but as a couple who had made mistakes. We came to realize that we were doing the seminars to help us practice what we are preaching.

The more seminars we did, the more flexible I became in relating to Brenda. We've been doing marriage seminars for about fifteen years, and I still have a lot to learn!

For me, the biggest reward is that Brenda is now my best friend. I can talk to her about anything. And I am not afraid to appear weak or to fail. She challenges me not to be content with failure, and she is my biggest fan and greatest critic. She is allowing me to dream my dreams and to make some of them a reality, such as writing books.

As I am learning how to help her feel more and more secure in our relationship, I reap the benefits of her blossoming. This security allows Brenda to demonstrate more of her spiritual gifts. More oneness is developing in our relationship, which helps us to be more patient with each other. As this takes place, it becomes more obvious why God put us together: He receives more glory with us together than He could from us separately.

Touching the Rim

Many years ago while playing basketball in college, I could not touch the rim, but I desperately wanted to. Steve Irwin, my basketball coach, had the team do some drills during our preseason, one of which was jumping trying to touch the rim. After several attempts one day, I barely touched the rim and became extremely excited. Coach Irwin demonstrated several weight-lifting drills, which isolated my thigh muscles. That was all the motivation I needed! It was not long before I could easily place my wrist over the rim. Eventually, I could take one step and grab the rim. This newfound skill was not just for show; it helped me in playing defense against taller opponents. I now had the ability to block their shots. But to be able to use this skill, I had to continually lift weights. If I stopped lifting weights, I lost my ability to jump.

This same principle can be transferred to marriage. I believe that if we see change in ourselves and our wives see change in us, this will motivate them and us to continue improving our marriages. And it will deepen our relationships as best friends.

Brenda and I continue to work at our marriage. The fact that we have room to grow in our relationship to each other means that we have room to become even closer, which is exciting. If I stop working on improving our marriage, our relationship will deteriorate.

IT'S WORTH IT

As I reflect on my fifteen years of marriage, I see that it has been worth all the struggles and effort invested. The returns, which are the richness of the relationship with my wife and children, are incredible! Let me encourage you to come to the same conclusion that I have: Your marriage is worth working through the struggles and hard work required to produce a healthy relationship with your wife.

I can't guarantee that if you do all that is written in this book that your wife will become your best friend. I have found that I can't change anyone, but I can allow God to change me. I strongly believe that if you allow God to change you and you begin to implement the principles I have discussed in this book, your wife will be positively affected. She will grow closer to you because you have lowered the barriers that may have kept you apart.

One of the themes of this book is that how we treat our wives will create either a good or a bad legacy for our children and their children. My prayer is that as my three girls see the way I treat their mother, it will inspire them to pray for and marry spiritually mature Christian men. This will give me a greater chance of having godly grandchildren.

But the influences of our marriages don't stop with our families. Our marriages influence the people at church, those in our neighborhood, and the people with whom we work.

What have you got to lose? If you haven't started already, then start now helping your wife become your best friend.

Summary Points

1. The strength of your marriage should be based not only on your love for each other, but on your love and obedience to Jesus Christ, your Savior.

2. Placing yourself ahead of the marriage causes you to work at cross-purposes with your wife, even when you love her deeply. Work toward becoming a teammate with her and work together, instead of independently of each other.

3. Working as a team will give you both greater joy and fulfillment, especially during trials, because you are both serving the same Master with the same goal. Both of you will feel more secure in obedience to God's plan for harmony in marriage, and you will be closer, becoming one in purpose.

4. A successful, happy marriage that honors God requires both partners to work at being servants to each other and acting out of selfless love in all that you do. In working to become one, you will find the rewards worth your labors.

Action Points

1. Are you obedient to Christ in all aspects of your life, including your marriage?

   Review your self-check answers from the previous chapters. Are there any unresolved questions of obedience to God's will for your success in your marriage?

2. Do you feel that you and your wife are a team? Or do you too often operate independently of one another?

   Examine ways that you can think and act more closely together.

   Plan times together to discuss things such as family budgets and major expenditures or policies on television watching for the children or the whole family. Make sure to apply the lessons of the servant-leader in talking with your wife.

3. In what areas do you and your wife work well together?

   What makes these partnering efforts successful?

Use these examples to build on in making all areas of your marriage a positive, teamwork-inspired effort.

4. Look at some long-lasting marriages in your family or at church. Talk to these husbands and ask them what they did to maintain these prosperous marriages. Does their advice coincide with what you have learned in this book?

Apply the pertinent lessons and principles of other successful marriages in building and strengthening your own marriage team.

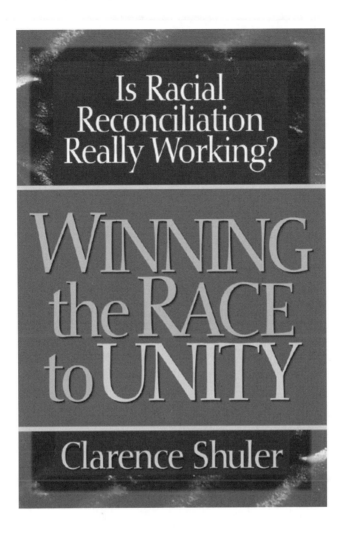

Winning the Race to Unity
Is Racial Reconciliation Really Working?
ISBN 0-8024-8199-X

It's been said that Sunday morning are the most segregated hours of the week. Why does the church still struggle with racial tension? Addressing both white and black believers, Clarence Shuler suggests practical, biblical ways to achieve racial harmony.

MOODY
The Name You Can Trust
1-800-678-8812 www.MoodyPress.org